MIRACLE MORNING MILLIONAIRES

What the Wealthy Do Before 8AM That Will Make You Rich

Hal Elrod • David Osborn

With Honorée Corder

Paperback ISBN: 978-1-942589-23-5
E book IBSN: 978-1-942589-24-2

Interior Design: Christina Gorchos, 3CsBooks.com

DEDICATION

Hal

This book is dedicated to the people who mean more to me than anything in the world—my family. Mom. Dad. My sister, Hayley. My wife, Ursula, and our two children—Sophie and Halsten. I love you all more than I can put into words!

This book is also in loving memory of my sister, Amery Kristine Elrod.

David

My family, especially my wife Traci, my Mom, my daughters Cheaven and Bella, and my son Luke. My team, for supporting our mission each and every day. All those who aspire for abundance, everywhere.

CONTENTS

PART I: The Miracle Morning

PART II: What Makes a Millionaire

PART III: Three Personal Growth Practices to Power your Path to Wealth

A SPECIAL INVITATION FROM HAL

Readers and practitioners of *The Miracle Morning* have co-created an extraordinary community consisting of over 150,000 like-minded individuals from around the world who wake up each day *with purpose* and dedicate time to fulfilling the unlimited potential that is within all of us, while helping others to do the same.

As author of *The Miracle Morning*, I felt that I had a responsibility to create an online community where readers could come together to connect, get encouragement, share best practices, support one another, discuss the book, post videos, find an accountability partner, and even swap smoothie recipes and exercise routines.

However, I honestly had no idea that The Miracle Morning Community would become one of the most positive, engaged, and supportive online communities in the world, but it has. I'm constantly astounded by the caliber and the character of our members, which presently includes people from over seventy countries and is growing daily.

Just go to **www.MyTMMCommunity.com** and request to join The Miracle Morning Community on Facebook. You'll immediately be able to connect with 150,000+ people who are already practicing TMM. While you'll find many who are just beginning their Miracle Morning journey, you'll find even more who have been at it for years and will happily share advice, support, and guidance to accelerate your success.

I moderate the Community and check in regularly, so I look forward to seeing you there! If you'd like to connect with me personally on social media, just follow **@HalElrod** on Twitter and **Facebook.com/YoPalHal** on Facebook. Let's connect soon!

HAL'S INTRODUCTION

MEET DAVID OSBORN

A few years ago, I was invited to speak at an event for the non-profit, *1 Life Fully Lived*. The featured speaker was someone I had not yet heard of, but the consensus amongst attendees at the event was that he would be the highlight of the event. I was intrigued.

When David Osborn took the stage, I was quickly captivated—as was everyone else in the room—by his rare blend of authenticity, transparency, expertise and contribution.

His message was titled *Wealth Can't Wait*, and he walked us through his story of going from a troubled youth to a self-made multi-millionaire. His transparency was encouraging, as he showed us where virtually every dollar he earned came from. And there were *a lot* of dollars—approximately 70 million of them, referring to his net worth at the time.

Up until that point, I had met a few millionaires, but none who were at that level. And none with such an openness and willingness to share what they knew—for free—in a sincere effort to help others achieve their own financial freedom. My intrigue grew.

During the course of David's presentation, I learned that he was also one of the co-founders of *GoBundance*—a mastermind for men who choose to lead epic lives. Wanting to get more time to connect with David, I accepted an offer to speak at the upcoming GoBundance retreat in Lake Tahoe. Little did I know that the GoBundance trip would present the beginning of an invaluable friendship between David and I, as well as our families.

Since that trip to Lake Tahoe, my family moved to Austin, Texas, living just 15 minutes away from David and his family. Our wives have become great friends. Our daughters are bestsies. Our kids attend the same school—a Montessori type school. Last week, they even bought a house down the street from us, so we'll soon be neighbors. At this rate, I think it may only be a matter of time before we're living together.

In October of 2016, when I was diagnosed with a rare form of cancer that came with a 30% survival rate, David and his wife, Traci, stepped up in vital ways to support me and my family. They had meals delivered to us every week, for over a year. They drove me to the hospital. They even offered to fly us anywhere we needed to go, on their plane. Having lost his father to cancer, David empathized and offered guidance based on his own journey. The phrase "I can never thank you enough" sums up the gratitude that I feel for David and his family.

I hope that gives you a better understanding of who you're about to learn from. I asked David to co-author this book with me, to bring you his wisdom, because he embodies what it means to me to be truly *wealthy*. Wealth is not just about the dollars in your bank account, or your net worth. True wealth is about living in alignment with what matters most to you—in alignment with your values, only one of which is about financial freedom. And nobody does that better than David Osborn.

DAVID'S INTRODUCTION

THE MORNING MILLIONAIRE

This morning I woke up at 5:17.

Believe me; I am *not* bragging. I spent a large part of my life as a self-proclaimed night owl. I fondly remember high school weekends when I could sleep until 10 or 11 a.m. In college, I'd sleep through classes, and when exams came, I'd study late into the night.

When I started running a business, I stuck with those same habits—working late while the world was asleep and then sleeping in. And why not? For me, nights were a productive time. But mornings? I spent them sleeping as late as the world would let me.

Of course, I quickly learned a couple of things.

The first was that the world wouldn't always *let* me sleep as late as I wanted. Most of the world runs on daylight, so as a night owl, my late nights tended to catch up to me. No matter how productive I thought I was at night, stumbling around my business during the day like a zombie was no shortcut to wealth.

Second, and arguably more important, I began to discover that *there is a connection between mornings and wealth.* Not only does the world rarely sleep in, but the millionaires of the world almost *never* do.

The Morning–Millionaire Connection

The more time I spent in business, the more I began to see the connection between mornings and money. The more consistently I leveraged that first part of my day—in very specific ways that I'll share with you—the more my net worth increased.

I'm not alone. If you look at the habits of millionaires, as we will throughout this book, you'll find that an unusual proportion of wealthy people wake up early. There's a good reason for that: mornings and money have a lot in common.

When it comes to money, perhaps the most popular personal financial advice in the world is to "pay yourself first"—to take some of the money that comes in, and *before anything else*, put that money aside to invest. The premise is that the most powerful financial tool in the world is compound interest, but if you never have any money to invest, you'll never get to take advantage of it. You have to take that money *first*; otherwise, it just gets consumed by other things.

Time is similar. Developing yourself is the most powerful tool in the world. As with money, promising yourself you'll set time aside *later* in the day to do what matters most just never seems to work— just as money will always find a new home, so will your time. By the last few dollars of your paycheck, it's too late to save; by noon, it's too late to do what's most important with your time.

Miracle Mornings are like paying yourself first—in wisdom, productivity, and clarity. When you leverage mornings, it's like you're skimming the cream off the top of the day and giving it to yourself so you can invest it for huge returns.

Of all the investments in the world, from real estate and annuities to stock markets and startups, the best investment is always *you*. And the tool to do that shows up every single day at sunrise, without fail.

Beginning Your Morning Journey

This book is about three things.

First, it's about identifying and teaching you the essential practices that define those people who choose to become wealthy. If you can learn those practices, you can follow in their footsteps. It's that simple. (No, it's not *easy*. But it is simple.)

Second, it's about understanding the value—and there's a lot of it—in making those practices the *very first thing you do each day*. Sure, you can try to do them later, but I suspect you know all too well where that road leads. As you'll discover, mornings have a special quality to them. They matter—in ways you may not yet be able to imagine. You won't become wealthy *just* by waking up early, but it's no exaggeration to say that mornings can make the difference between being broke and being a millionaire.

Finally, this book is about learning the boots-on-the-ground, practical skills of becoming that rare creature known as a "morning person." I can tell you over and over how critical mornings are, but if you can't wake up early enough to take advantage of them, none of this matters. The good news is that *being a morning person is a skill you can learn*. You really *can* become a morning person. You can wake up excited and energetic. *You* can be the early bird. It's my job to show you how.

These three things can profoundly change how you experience the world—and not just in terms of wealth. When you take control of your mornings, you take control of your days. You get to engage with the world under your terms. You can act, instead of *react*.

Imagine a day where *you* set the agenda. One where the things that matter to you are clear and the steps ahead are exciting. That's what the Miracle Morning offers you—not just the possibility of financial wealth but also an abundance of peace and a sense of control over your life.

Our starting point for this journey is to learn to take advantage of your mornings right away—starting tomorrow, in fact. Beginning with mornings means that you can start leveraging that important part of the day right away while you continue to work through this book and learn exactly how millionaires became wealthy.

As we get started, remember that *mornings are where the magic is.* It's where you develop the mindset to become wealthy and where you turn your dreams, your passions and your talents to the business of becoming a millionaire. Mornings are where it all begins.

If this makes you nervous, fear not. Even if you've struggled with mornings in the past, take this to heart: the problem you have with mornings isn't the morning itself. It's the rest of your day. If you aren't satisfied with your life, there's no reason to jump out of bed full of energy. You might say there's no reason to get out of bed at *all*. Which is, I think, how a lot of people feel, and why a lot of people struggle to wake up.

That's why our journey together begins with interrupting that cycle. We'll start with why mornings matter so much, and then we'll teach you how to wake up and take advantage of them as a daily part of your journey to wealth.

Many people tend to think, "I'll fix my life, then I'll want to get up early," or, "Once I'm wealthy, I'll change my habits." I can tell you with confidence that the causation runs in the other direction: you don't become a morning person by fixing your life; you fix your life one morning at a time.

If you're willing to choose to have more in your life—more productive mornings and more wealth—but aren't sure how to do it, this is the book for you. As long as you're willing to choose more, this book will help you *get* more.

Welcome to *Miracle Morning Millionaires.* Let's get started.

PART I:

THE MIRACLE MORNING

WHY MORNINGS MATTER, AND HOW YOU CAN TAKE THEM BACK

—1—
WHY MORNINGS MATTER
(MORE THAN YOU THINK)

*"You've got to wake up every morning with determination
if you're going to go to bed with satisfaction."*

–GEORGE LORIMER,
American journalist and author

After spending much of my early life sleeping in, it's now a miracle of sorts if I'm still asleep at 7 a.m. Even after a late night, I'm usually up early—the habit is just part of me now.

What first "flipped" my schedule was the realization that, as my responsibilities grew, the strategy of sleeping in and working late simply wasn't working. It wasn't functional. I couldn't stay up late at night to be productive and also be up early the next morning to engage with my family, run a business, and interact with a world that increasingly demanded that I stop being a vampire.

That realization was the catalyst for change—I reluctantly became a morning person out of sheer necessity. But, as I soon discovered, there was far more to mornings than just getting up early enough to tackle a busy life. Mornings, I began to realize, were like a hidden secret that I'd been missing for years. They didn't just allow me to do more—they allowed me to do things that I otherwise couldn't accomplish at *all.*

Now, many years and many dollars later, my Miracle Morning routine isn't something I have to do; it's what I *want* to do. I'm not quite sure how I'd live my life without it.

Right Foot, Wrong Foot

Part of the magic of mornings is that they set the tone for the rest of your day. Start every day with a purposeful, disciplined, and growth-infused morning, and you'll find that your day follows suit. You'll feel purposeful and on track. You'll be goal-oriented and less easily distracted. When you get mornings right, you're virtually guaranteed to crush your day.

Contrast that with what your morning probably looks like now. Most people fall into one of two morning camps. The first is *overwhelm.* From the moment you (reluctantly) wake up, you're frantically playing catch-up, running late, your mind racing. You're not even wearing pants yet, and you're already late. There's always so much to do but too little time to do it.

The other morning camp is *underwhelm.* Lacking goals and drive, you sleep in, procrastinate and finally, *finally,* start work. But even then, you're easily distracted by the slightest flash of something shiny, and you never feel like you're doing anything productive. You're drifting. Aimless.

For the overwhelmers, the day feels like one long fire drill. Chaos, noise, and an ever-present sense of rushing. For the underwhelmers, the day is like the world's slowest car crash, where you have no idea which pedals to push or how to turn the steering wheel to stop the impending doom.

But for both camps, there's always the looming question of money. The pressure of never having enough, of wondering where it's going to come from. Of feeling helpless to control your financial future.

Financial pressure is like an extra layer of stress that coats everything in your day.

In either case, when you don't take advantage of mornings, by the time you wake up, the world is already coming at you. If you start the day late, your day has already *blown* up by the time you wake up. If you wake up without any goals or direction, your days are practically guaranteed to get you nowhere. No matter which of those ways your morning starts, it's enough to make anyone want to stay in bed.

But what if there was a third option?

What if your morning was different? What if it *felt* different? What if you could wake up with energy and enthusiasm, instead of dread? What if, instead of chaos, you could have an hour of peace and quiet dedicated to improving yourself, your finances, and your life?

With Miracle Mornings, that clean, uncluttered mental space you've imagined is right there for the taking. A space where you can regain your sense of elegance and dignity, where you're in total control and can begin to create the life you dream of.

Why Mornings Matter So Much

My experience has been that the more you explore the power of early rising and morning rituals, the better poised you are to build purposeful wealth. But don't take my word for it—there's increasing evidence that the early bird gets a lot more than the worm. Here are just a few of the key advantages you're about to experience for yourself when you create your Miracle Morning:

- **You'll be more proactive and productive.** Christoph Randler is a professor of biology at the Heidelberg University of Education in Heidelberg, Germany. In the July 2010 issue of Harvard Business Review, Randler found that "people whose performance peaks in the morning are better positioned for career success because they're more proactive than people who are at their best in the evening." According to *New York Times* bestselling author and world-renowned entrepreneur Robin

Sharma, "If you study many of the most productive people in the world, they all had one thing in common—they were early risers."

- **You'll anticipate problems and head them off at the pass.** Randler went on to surmise that morning people hold all of the important cards. They are "better able to anticipate and minimize problems, are proactive, have greater professional success and ultimately make higher wages." He noted that morning people are able to anticipate problems and handle them with grace and ease. And that means mornings can be the key to decreasing the level of stress that inevitably comes from the unexpected emergencies ranging from kids and work to relationships and money.

- **You'll plan like a pro.** It's been said that when we fail to plan, we are planning to fail. That's even truer when it comes to wealth. Morning folks not only have the time to organize, anticipate, and prepare for their day, they also have time to financially plan. Our sleepy counterparts are reactive, leaving a lot to chance. Aren't you more stressed when you sleep through your alarm? Getting up with the sun (or before) lets you jump-start your day. While everyone else is running around trying (and failing) to get their day under control, you'll have a far better shot at staying calm, cool, and collected, following your plan.

- **You'll have more energy.** One component of your new Miracle Mornings will be morning exercise, which often is something neglected by…well, just about everyone. As little as a few *minutes* of exercise sets a positive tone for the day. Increased blood to the brain will help you think more clearly and focus on what's most important. Fresh oxygen will permeate every cell in your body and increase your energy, which is why people who exercise are in better moods and better shape, get better sleep, and become more productive.

- **You'll gain early bird attitude advantages.** Recently, researchers at the University of Barcelona in Spain compared morning people—those early birds who like to get up at dawn—with evening people: night owls who prefer to stay up late and sleep in. Among the differences they found were that morning people tend to be more persistent and resistant to fatigue, frustration, and difficulties. That translates into decreased anxiety, depression and likelihood of substance abuse, and higher life satisfaction.

The evidence is in, and the experts have had their say: mornings matter—for almost everything. I can tell you from the perspective of someone who's built wealth that each one of those benefits is an enormous advantage on the journey to becoming a millionaire. Look at the list:

- Productivity
- Proactive problem solving
- Higher income
- Daily planning
- Higher energy
- More positive mood and resilience

Is there a better list of traits needed to become wealthy? I don't think so. And every one of them is connected, *by research*, to mornings.

At this point, then, there should be no doubt that mornings have a certain magical quality. Your burning question should be this:

If mornings are so great, why aren't we all up early?

It's not only an insightful question, but it's also one we have to answer before you can truly start to implement the five-step morning wake-up process in chapter 2.

The Real Trouble with Mornings

If you've struggled with mornings, you know from experience that willpower and enthusiasm at bedtime has an insidious way of abandoning you when your alarm goes off the next morning.

You're not alone here. Waking up earlier is just one of many New Year's resolutions that tend to fail early and fail often. To be successful in the transition, you need to understand a few truths about waking up early that you may not have considered. They're the truths that underlie the five-step approach to waking up that you're going to use starting tomorrow.

1. Your sleep behavior is habitual.

Are some people naturally drawn to nights and others to mornings? I think so, and research supports this. But that predisposition is also just that—it's a *tendency* in most people, not a genetic prophecy. What is also at play is the simple fact that you have a lot of habits around sleep. You've almost certainly been doing the same things at night and in the morning for *years*. Anything you do that consistently for that long becomes a habit.

Habits are powerful forces. When you struggle to open your eyes as your alarm screams on your bedside table, it's important to remember that part of what you're fighting is the neural patterns in your brain that keep you doing the same things, without really thinking about it.

The good news is that you can change your habits. Waking up early is a *skill*—you can learn it, just like you can learn to ride a bike or run a business. And you'll learn exactly how in the chapters ahead.

2. How you wake up is influenced by the day ahead.

Have you ever had the experience of retreating under the covers for "just a little more sleep" because you knew you had to do something hard, boring, or emotionally demanding that day?

Waking up for a day you're excited about is a different experience than waking up for one that you dread. Even early birds retreat under the covers when they dread the day ahead.

The Miracle Morning approach tackles this in two ways. First, by giving you something to look forward to each morning: controlled, personal time to improve your finances, your health, your mood, and your life.

Second, the more often you use your mornings this way, the better the days ahead start to look! As your Miracle Morning benefits kick in, you'll begin to make changes in your life that make those retreats under the covers less and less frequent.

3. You're worried about being selfish.

One of the barriers to waking up early, surprisingly, isn't just the battle to escape your bed. It's a sneaky form of self-sabotage that tells us, *spending that time on yourself every day is selfish.*

Many of us have been taught that success means putting our own needs last. You should, we're told, take care of your family, your job, your community, and *then* yourself. If there's time. The problem is that what we put off often gets *shut off.* We have so much to do that we never get to our own needs. Over time, we end up exhausted, depressed, resentful and overwhelmed.

Sound familiar?

I'm a firm believer in the advice given at the start of every airplane flight: put your oxygen mask on first and then help others. You won't be able to help anyone if you pass out due to lack of oxygen.

The same is true of your personal development and, through that, your wealth. Completely neglecting yourself is a recipe for financially "passing out." Remember:

- You can't help anyone if your life is self-destructing.
- You can't be productive if your health is spiraling downward.
- You can't build wealth if you don't take the time to learn, to develop the skills you need, and to create the mindset required to reach your financial goals.

The daily-life equivalent of putting on your mask first is *using the morning.* Mornings are the key to all of it. Mornings are where you take control and chart the course for the life you truly want.

You're the pilot of the flight. No one else is going to grab the controls but *you.* And you can't do that if you're asleep.

These three things, more than anything else, are the demons you're attempting to slay as you begin to create your Miracle Morning. The good news is that, like millions of other people, you can do it.

Mornings? Really?

Right now, there may be a voice in your head saying, *Riiiiight.*

That's your inner morning skeptic, and believe me, I understand. I've been there. The first response to this is often that it sounds great *in theory.* "But," you think, "there is no way. I'm already cramming twenty-seven hours of stuff into twenty-four hours. How on earth could I get up an hour earlier than I already do?"

I ask the question, "How can you *not*?" Mornings can transform your life. They can be the worst part of your day, or they can become a true miracle.

If you're skeptical, the key point to understand is that the Miracle Morning isn't about denying yourself another hour of sleep so you can have a longer, harder day. It's not even about waking up earlier. It's about waking up *better.*

Tens of thousands of people around the planet are already living their Miracle Mornings. Many of them were once night owls. But they are making it work, and they're *thriving.* And it's not because they added an hour to their day. It's because they added the *right* hour. And so can you. (If you're convinced you don't have time, hang in there: in chapter 3, I'll show you a format for a *six-minute* Miracle Morning. Who doesn't have six minutes?)

If you're still skeptical, let me tell you this: the hardest part about getting up an hour earlier—or any amount earlier—is the first five minutes. That's the crucial time when, tucked into your warm bed, you make the decision to start your day or hit the snooze button just one more time. It's the moment of truth, and the decision you make right then will change your day, your success, and your life.

That's why the first five minutes is the starting point for *The Miracle Morning for Millionaires.* When we win our mornings, we win the day, and it's time for you to win *every* morning!

Take it from a former night owl: getting from "I'm not a morning person" to "Good day, sunshine!" is a process. But after some trial and error, you will discover how to outfox your inner late sleeper so you can make early rising a habit.

Mornings don't just matter. They matter more than you can possibly imagine right now. They truly do have the power to transform your life.

In the next two chapters, I'll make waking up early easier and more exciting than it's ever been in your life—even if you've never considered yourself to be a morning person. And I'll show you how to maximize those newfound morning minutes with six of most powerful, proven personal development practices in history.

೮౩

Morning Millionaires

Over my 50 years in business, I have learned that if I rise early I can achieve so much more in a day, and therefore in life…

No matter where I am in the world, I try to routinely wake up at around 5 a.m. By rising early, I'm able to do some exercise and spend time with my family, which puts me in a great mind frame before getting down to business…

Being an early riser isn't about trumpeting how hard you work. It's about doing everything within your power to help your business achieve success; and if that means you have to get up at an hour not known to most, then you might as well enjoy the sunrise.

—Richard Branson

IT ONLY TAKES FIVE MINUTES TO BECOME A MORNING PERSON

If you really think about it, hitting the snooze button in the morning doesn't even make sense. It's like saying, "I hate getting up in the morning, so I do it over, and over, and over again."

—DEMETRI MARTIN, Comedian

If I've done my job, then right now you should be feeling optimistic and even *excited* about tomorrow morning. You might be imagining how you're going to leap out of bed first thing in the morning and the layer of dust your snooze button is going to collect from lack of use.

But what happens tomorrow morning when that alarm goes off? How motivated will you be when you're yanked out of a deep sleep by a screaming alarm clock? How excited will you be to get out of a warm bed in a cold house?

We all know where your motivation will be right then: flushed down the toilet. It will be replaced by the sneaky companion of lost mornings that's been around since the dawn of time: *rationalization*.

Rationalization is a crafty master. What seemed like a foregone conclusion the night before—to get up early and seize the day—can quickly vanish when morning comes. In seconds, you can convince yourself that you need just a few extra minutes of sleep and the next thing you know, you're scrambling around the house, late for work, late for life. Again.

It's a tricky problem. Just when we need our motivation the most—those first few moments of the day—is precisely when we seem to have the least of it.

But what if, tomorrow morning, you could tap into some of the momentum and enthusiasm you feel right *now*? That's our goal in this chapter—to boost your morning motivation and mount a surprise attack on rationalization.

Each of the five steps in the process that follows is designed to increase what Hal calls your Wake-Up Motivation Level (WUML). The higher your WUML, the more likely you are to dodge the snooze button and get up. Your job is to get your WUML above the snooze threshold by whatever means necessary.

Fortunately, the necessary means aren't as drastic or as difficult as you might imagine.

The Five-Step Snooze-Proof Wake-Up Strategy

You might feel that you have a low WUML, meaning that most mornings you want nothing more than to go back to sleep when your alarm goes off. That's normal. But by using the simple five-step, five-minute process in this chapter, you can crank up your WUML to the point that you're ready to jump up and embrace the day.

Five steps, five minutes. That's all it takes.

Minute One: Set Your Intentions Before Bed

The first key to waking up is to understand that *your first thought in the morning is usually the same as your last thought was before you went to sleep.* I bet, for example, that you've had nights where you could hardly fall asleep because you were so excited about waking up the next morning. Whether it was when you were a kid on Christmas morning or the day you were leaving for a big vacation, as soon as the alarm clock sounded, you opened your eyes ready to jump out of bed and embrace the day. Why? It's because the last thought you had about the coming morning—before you fell asleep—was positive.

On the other hand, if your last thought before bed was something like: *I can't believe I have to get up in six hours—I'm going to be exhausted in the morning,* then your first thought when the alarm clock goes off is likely to be something like, *Oh, gosh, it's already been six hours? Nooo… I just want to keep sleeping!*

Part of how you wake up in the morning, in other words, is a self-fulfilling prophecy. *You*, not your alarm, are creating your morning reality.

The first step, then, is to consciously decide—every night, before bed—to actively and mindfully create a positive expectation for the next morning. Visualize it and affirm it to yourself.

For help on this and to get the precise words to say before bed to create your powerful morning intentions, download Hal's very own *Bedtime Affirmations*, free, at www.TMMBook.com.

Minute Two: Get Out of Bed to Turn Your Alarm Off

If you haven't already, be sure to move your alarm clock as far away from your bed as possible. This means that you'll *have* to get out of bed and engage your body in movement first thing. Motion creates energy, so getting out of bed and walking across the room naturally helps you to wake up.

Most people keep their alarm clock next to their bed, within reach. That's perfect if you want to go back to sleep. But those first few moments of waking up are when your WUML is at its lowest point, which makes it much more difficult to summon the discipline to get out of bed. An alarm clock within arm's reach is a recipe for more snoozing. In fact, you may turn off the alarm without even realizing it! On more than a few occasions, we've all convinced ourselves that our alarm clock was merely part of the dream we were having. (You're not alone on that one, trust me.)

By forcing yourself to get out of bed to turn off the alarm clock, you are setting yourself up for early-rising success by instantly increasing your WUML.

However, on a scale of one to ten, your WUML may be hovering around a five, and you'll likely be feeling sleepier than not, so the temptation to turn around and crawl back into bed will still be present. You'll need to raise that WUML just a little further by immediately moving on to the next step:

Minute Three: Brush Your Teeth

As soon as you've gotten out of bed and turned off your alarm clock, go directly to the bathroom sink to brush your teeth. I know what you may be thinking: "Really? You're telling me that I need to brush my teeth?" Yes. The point here is that you're doing mindless activities for the first few minutes and giving your body time to wake up.

After turning off your alarm clock, go directly to the bathroom sink to brush your teeth, splash some warm (or, better yet, cold) water on your face. This simple activity will allow for the passing of more time to increase your WUML even further.

Now that your mouth is minty-fresh, it's time for:

Minute Four: Drink a Full Glass of Water

It's crucial that you hydrate yourself first thing every morning. After six to eight hours without water, you'll be mildly dehydrated, which causes fatigue. Often, when people feel tired—at any time of the day—what they need is more water, not more sleep.

Start by getting a glass or bottle of water (or you can do what we do and fill it up the night before, so it's already there for you in the morning) and drink it as fast as is comfortable for you. The objective is to replace the water you were deprived of during the hours you slept.

That glass of water should raise your WUML another notch, which will get you to:

Minute Five: Get Dressed in Your Workout Clothes (or Jump in the Shower)

The fifth step has two options. Option one is to get dressed in your exercise clothing, so you're ready to leave your bedroom and immediately engage in your Miracle Morning. You can either lay out your clothes before you go to bed or even sleep in your workout clothes. (Yes, really.)

Option two is to jump in the shower, which is a great way to take your WUML to the point where staying awake is much easier. However, I usually opt to change into exercise clothes, since I'll need a shower after working out or walking the dog. But many people prefer the morning shower because it helps them wake up and gives them a fresh start to the day. The choice is completely yours. If option one doesn't work, go for the shower option. That makes it *very* hard to go back to sleep.

Regardless of which option you choose, by the time you've executed these five simple steps, your WUML should be high enough that it requires very little discipline to stay awake for your Miracle Morning.

Contrast that with trying to make that commitment the moment your alarm clock first goes off, while you're at a WUML of nearly zero—it's a much more difficult decision to make. The five steps let you build momentum so that, within just a few minutes, you've escaped the gravitational field of rationalization, and you're ready to go instead of feeling groggy.

I've never made it through these first five minutes and *then* decided to go back to bed. Once I'm up and moving intentionally through the morning, it is much easier to continue being purposeful throughout the day.

Miracle Morning Bonus Wake-Up Tips

Although this strategy has worked for thousands of people, these five steps are not the only ways to make waking up in the morning easier. Here are a few others I've heard from fellow Miracle Morning practitioners:

- *Use the Miracle Morning Bedtime Affirmations.* If you haven't done this yet, you can go to www.TMMbook.com and download and print Hal's word-for-word Bedtime Affirmations. Keep these next to your bed to help you set your intentions each night before you fall asleep. These are designed to program your subconscious mind so that you're more easily able to beat the snooze button and wake up feeling energized.

- *Set a timer for your bedroom lights.* One member of The Miracle Morning Community shared that he sets his bedroom lights on a timer (you can buy an appliance timer online or at your local hardware store). As his alarm goes off, the lights come on in the room. What a great idea! It's a lot easier to fall back asleep when it's dark—having the lights on tells your mind and body that it's time to wake up. (Whether you use a timer or not, be sure to turn your light on right after you turn your alarm off.)

- *Set a timer for your bedroom heater.* Another member of The Miracle Morning Community says that in the winter, she keeps a bedroom heater on an appliance timer set to turn on fifteen minutes before she wakes up. She sets the temperature to be colder at night, but warmer for waking up, so she won't be tempted to crawl back under her covers.

Feel free to add to or customize the Five-Minute Snooze-Proof Wake-Up Strategy, and if you have any tips that you are open to sharing, we'd love to hear them. Please post them in The Miracle Morning Community at www.MyTMMCommunity.com.

Take Immediate Action!

It's decision time.

This is a critical turning point for you as a *Miracle Morning* reader. It's time to decide whether you're going to commit to discovering the power of mornings.

You now have a choice before you. Tomorrow morning, you can wake up early and inspired and begin to recreate your life—to start closing that gap between the life you're living and the life of financial abundance that you want.

Or you can do what you've always done and hope for the best.

If you're ready, you can start right *now*. Remember that waking up consistently and easily is all about having an effective, predetermined, step-by-step strategy to increase your WUML in the morning. Don't wait! You can do the following three steps right away—there's no need to wait for morning or bedtime:

1. *Set your alarm right now for thirty to sixty minutes earlier than you usually wake up and commit to leaving it there for the next thirty days.* That's it—just thirty to sixty minutes for thirty days, starting now. And be sure to write into your schedule to do your first Miracle Morning *tomorrow morning.* That's right; don't use waiting until you finish the book as an excuse to procrastinate on getting started!

2. *Join The Miracle Morning Community at www. MyTMMCommunity.com.* That's where you can connect with and get support from more than 200,000 like-minded early risers, many of whom have been generating extraordinary results with the Miracle Morning for years.

3. *Find a Miracle Morning accountability partner.* Enroll someone—your spouse, a friend, family member, coworker, or someone you meet in The Miracle Morning Community— to join you on this adventure so you can encourage, support, and hold each other accountable to follow through until your Miracle Morning has become a lifelong habit.

If you are feeling resistant, it may be because you've tried to make changes in the past but haven't followed through. Here's a suggestion: turn now to "Chapter 13: The 30-Day Miracle Morning Challenge." This chapter will give you the mindset and strategy to overcome any resistance you may have to getting started, plus it will give you the most effective process for implementing a new habit and sticking with it. It's the first journey you're going to embark on when the book is finished, and you can take a sneak peek now. Think of it as beginning with the end in mind.

Your First Investment Lesson

The previous chapter should give you serious pause for thought as to the value of mornings. All the evidence—and the words of thousands of people who have become Miracle Morning believers—point to a powerful idea:

What if mornings weren't how you *start* your day, but how you *create* it?

How you start your day could be the single most important factor in determining how you live your life. When you wake up with excitement and create a purposeful, powerful, productive morning, you set yourself up to win the day.

Yet, most people start their day by procrastinating, hitting the snooze button and waiting until the last possible moment to pry themselves out from beneath their cozy covers. While it may not be obvious, this seemingly innocent act may be sending a detrimental message to our subconscious. It programs our psyche with the unconscious belief that we don't have the self-discipline to get out of bed in the morning, let alone do what's necessary to achieve everything else we want for our lives—including building financial abundance.

When the alarm clock starts beeping in the morning, consider it life's first investment opportunity each day. It's the gift of another day, the challenge of making the disciplined decision to get out of bed, and the opportunity to invest time into our personal development, so each of us can become the person we need to be to create the life we want. And we get to do all of this while the rest of the world continues to sleep.

This is your first investment lesson on the road to wealth: maintaining discipline for just a few moments each morning—the first few moments when you decide to get up rather than stay in bed—is a discipline that can pay dividends for the rest of your life.

* * *

When people ask me how I transformed myself into a morning person—and transformed my life in the process—I tell them I did it in five simple steps, one at a time. Five simple, snooze-proof keys that made waking up in the morning—even *early* in the morning—easier than ever before. Without this strategy, I would still be sleeping (or snoozing) through the alarm(s) each morning. Worse, I would still be clinging to the limiting belief that I am not a morning person.

And I would have missed a whole world of opportunity.

I know it may seem downright impossible. But take it from a former snooze-aholic: you can do this. And you can do it the same way I did.

That's the critical message about waking up—*it's possible to change.* Like most millionaires, most morning people aren't born—they're self-made. You can do it, and it doesn't require the willpower of an Olympic marathoner. I contend that when early rising becomes not only something you do but who you *are,* you will truly love mornings. Waking up will become as effortless for you as it is for me.

Not convinced? Suspend your disbelief a little and try the five-step process tomorrow. It might change your life the way it changed mine. From this day forward, starting with the next thirty days, keep your alarm set for thirty to sixty minutes earlier so that you can start waking up when you want to, instead of when you have to. It's time to start launching each day with a Miracle Morning so that you can become the person you need to be to take yourself, your children, and your family to extraordinary levels.

What will you do with that hour? You're going to find out in the next chapter, but for now, continue reading this book during your Miracle Morning until you learn the whole routine.

❧

Morning Millionaires

Ninety-five percent of the time I get eight hours of sleep a night, and as a result, ninety-five percent of the time I don't need an alarm to wake up. And waking up naturally is, for me, a great way to start the day.

A big part of my morning ritual is about what I don't do: when I wake up, I don't start the day by looking at my smartphone. Instead, once I'm awake, I take a minute to breathe deeply, be grateful, and set my intention for the day.

I've made small changes over time; for example, when I lived in Los Angeles I was fond of morning walks and hikes. I'm very open to experimenting - I'm sure before long I'll learn about something new I'll want to add to my routine.

And no, I don't believe in the snooze button. On days when I have to use my alarm, I always set it for the last possible moment I have to get up.

—Arianna Huffington

— 3 —
THE LIFE S.A.V.E.R.S.
Six Practices Guaranteed to Save You from a Life of Unfulfilled Potential

Going through S.A.V.E.R.S. every morning is like pumping rocket fuel into my body, mind, and spirit ... before I start my day, every day.

—ROBERT KIYOSAKI, Best-Selling author of *Rich Dad Poor Dad*

When Hal experienced the second of his two rock bottoms (the first was when he died for six minutes in a car crash, and the second was when his business failed due to the financial collapse of 2008), he felt lost and depressed. Applying what he already knew, wasn't working. Nothing he tried improved his situation. So, he began his quest for the fastest, most effective strategy to take his success to the next level. He went in search of the best personal development practices, the ones used by the world's most successful people.

That search led Hal to a list of six of the most timeless, proven personal development practices on the planet. They were the ones that delivered the best results, consistently, for the people who used them.

At first, Hal tried to determine which one or two would accelerate his success the fastest. His breakthrough came, however, when he asked himself a simple question: *what would happen if I did ALL of these?*

So, he did. Within just two months of implementing all six practices nearly every single day, Hal experienced what you might call "miraculous" results. He was able to more than double his income, and he went from someone who hated running and had never run more than a mile to training to run a 52-mile ultramarathon. Those six practices not only pulled him out of his rock bottom but turned out to be the best way to take his physical, mental, emotional, and spiritual capacities to another level.

I had a similar breakthrough in business. There was no car crash, thankfully, but it was no less transformational. I had already discovered that taking control of my mornings was directly connected to increasing my wealth, but what made the difference was not just waking up early. It was waking up and doing *very specific things.* The connection between mornings and my millionaire status was directly related to the six practices—a morning process Hal calls the Life S.A.V.E.R.S.

Let's recap. We've made a case for why mornings matter. We've given you the tools to begin your transition to becoming a morning person.

The obvious question now is, *what do you do with that time?*

This chapter is the answer to that question.

Why the S.A.V.E.R.S. Work

The S.A.V.E.R.S. are simple but profoundly effective daily morning practices that are virtually guaranteed to help you develop yourself. They give you the space you need to gain real clarity—a kind of high-level, minutiae-free view where you can plan and live your life on your terms. The S.A.V.E.R.S. are designed to put you in a peak physical, mental, emotional, and spiritual state each morning—a state in which you'll continually improve, consistently feel great, and always perform at your best.

I know what you're thinking: *I don't have time. How can I do six more things when I can barely get out the door each morning?*

Trust me; I've been there. Before the Miracle Morning, I often woke up to pure chaos. Like you, I barely had enough time to get dressed, fed, and out the door for the first obligation of the day.

It may seem like you can hardly squeeze in what you have to do already, never mind what you want to do. But I "didn't have time" before the Miracle Morning, either. And yet, here I am with more time, more prosperity, and more peace than I've ever had before.

Here's the secret that you have to experience for yourself: *your Miracle Morning will create time for you.* The Life S.A.V.E.R.S. are the vehicle to help you reconnect with your true essence and wake up with purpose instead of obligation. The practices help you to see priorities more clearly and find the most productive flow in your life. When you spend more time in that state, you get more done each day, you have fewer emergencies, and you have more energy.

In other words, the Life S.A.V.E.R.S. don't take time from your day but ultimately add more to it.

Each letter in S.A.V.E.R.S. represents one of the best practices of the most successful people on the planet. From A-list movie stars and world-class professional athletes to CEOs and entrepreneurs, you'd be hard-pressed to find an elite performer that doesn't swear by at least one of the S.A.V.E.R.S.

That's what makes the Miracle Morning so effective: you harness the game-changing benefits of not just one, but all six of the best practices, cultivated over centuries of human consciousness development and combined into a concise, fully customizable morning ritual.

The S.A.V.E.R.S. are:

Silence

Affirmations

Visualization

Exercise

Reading

Scribing

Take it from me: the S.A.V.E.R.S. are a profoundly powerful tool for developing wealth. Leveraging these six practices will accelerate your personal development by maximizing the impact of your newfound Miracle Morning ritual. They're customizable to fit you, your lifestyle, your business, and your specific goals. And you can start implementing them first thing tomorrow morning.

Let's go through each of the S.A.V.E.R.S. in detail.

S is for Silence

Most people start their day the way I used to: when their alarm tells them to. For them—and perhaps you—the very first sound of the day is the jarring squeal of their phone or clock.

From there, it's on to more "noise": a reach for the nearest screen where the racket of email, phone calls, social media, text messages and the news of the day awaits.

When you take the time to step back and look at it, is it any wonder we spend our days running from morning to night, struggling to regain control? Is it any surprise that we feel overwhelmed?

The first of the S.A.V.E.R.S. is *silence*, and it's your opportunity to learn the power of beginning each day with peaceful, purposeful quiet that will immediately reduce your stress levels and bring you the clarity you need to focus on what's most important.

Silence, of course, isn't another word for *nothing*. Far from it. The silence of your Miracle Morning is deliberate, and you have many choices for your personal practice. In no particular order, here are a few to get you started:

- Meditation
- Prayer
- Reflection
- Deep breathing
- Gratitude

Many of the world's most successful people are daily practitioners of silence. It's not surprising that Oprah practices stillness—or that she does nearly all of the other Life S.A.V.E.R.S., too. Musician Katy Perry practices Transcendental Meditation, as do Sheryl Crow and Sir Paul McCartney. Film and television stars Jennifer Aniston, Ellen DeGeneres, Jerry Seinfeld, Howard Stern, Cameron Diaz, Clint Eastwood, and Hugh Jackman have all spoken of their daily meditation practice. Even famous billionaires Ray Dalio and Rupert Murdoch have attributed their financial success to the daily practice of stillness. You'll be in good (and quiet) company by doing the same.

In an interview with *Shape* magazine, actress and singer Kristen Bell said, "Do meditative yoga for ten minutes every morning. When you have a problem—whether it's road rage, your guy, or work— meditation allows everything to unfold the way it's supposed to."

And don't be afraid to expand your horizons. Meditation comes in many forms. As Angelina Jolie told *Stylist* magazine, "I find meditation in sitting on the floor with the kids coloring for an hour or going on the trampoline. You do what you love, that makes you happy, and that gives you your meditation."

The Benefits of Silence

Stress is one of the most common side effects of a busy life, and it's no less present on the road to wealth. There are the ever-present distractions of other people encroaching on your schedule, and the inevitable fires to extinguish. There are co-workers, employees, and family—all of whom have the uncanny ability to push your buttons. And those buttons are all the more sensitive when you start your day in a rush.

Excessive stress is terrible for your health. It triggers your fight-or-flight response, releasing a cascade of toxic hormones that can stay in your body for days. According to PsychologyToday.com, "The stress hormone, cortisol, is public health enemy number one. Scientists have known for years that elevated cortisol levels interfere with learning and memory, lower immune function and bone density, increase weight gain, blood pressure, cholesterol, heart disease... The list goes on and on. Chronic stress and elevated cortisol levels also increase risk for depression, mental illness, and lower life expectancy."

It's fine if you experience that type of stress only occasionally, but many of us are under that kind of stress almost all the time. How many times a day do you find yourself in stressful situations? How many times do you have to deal with immediate needs that take you away from your vision or plan? If your day is one long cortisol release, starting your morning with a quiet moment is your first line of defense.

Silence in the form of meditation lowers your cortisol levels, which reduces stress and improves your health. A major study run by several groups, including the National Institutes of Health, the American Medical Association, the Mayo Clinic, and scientists from both Harvard and Stanford, revealed that meditation reduces stress and high blood pressure. A recent study by Dr. Norman Rosenthal, a world-renowned psychiatrist who works with the David Lynch Foundation, even found that people who practice meditation are 30 percent less likely to die from heart disease.

Another study from Harvard found that just eight weeks of meditation could lead to "increased gray-matter density in the hippocampus, known to be important for learning and memory, and in structures associated with self-awareness, compassion, and introspection."

Meditation helps you to slow down and focus on you, even if it's for just a short time. "I started meditating because I felt like I needed to stop my life from running me," singer Sheryl Crow has said. "So, meditation for me helped slow my day down." She continues to devote twenty minutes in the morning and twenty minutes at night to meditation.

Silence opens a space for you to secure your oxygen mask before assisting others. Practicing silence can bring you clarity and peace of mind, help you reduce your stress, improve your cognitive performance, and increase your confidence at the same time.

Guided Meditations and Meditation Apps

Meditation is like anything else—if you've never done it before, then it can be difficult or feel awkward at first. If you are a first-time meditator, I recommend starting with a guided meditation.

Here are a few of my favorite meditation apps that are available for both iPhone/iPad and Android devices:

- Headspace
- Calm
- Omvana
- Simply Being
- Insight Timer
- Oak

There are subtle and significant differences among these meditation apps, one of which is the voice of the person speaking.

If you don't have a device that allows you to download apps, go to YouTube or Google and search for the keywords "guided meditation." You can also search by duration (i.e. "five-minute guided meditation") or topic (i.e. "guided meditation for increased confidence").

Miracle Morning (Individual) Meditation

When you're ready to try meditating on your own, here is a simple, step-by-step meditation you can use during your Miracle Morning, even if you've never done this before.

Before beginning, it's important to prepare yourself and set expectations. This is a time for you to quiet your mind and let go of the compulsive need to be constantly thinking about something—reliving the past or worrying about the future, but never living fully in the present. This is the time to let go of your stresses, take a break from worrying about your problems, and be here in this moment. It is a time to access the essence of who you are—to go deeper than what you have, what you do, or the labels you've accepted as who you are.

If this sounds foreign to you, or too New Age-y, that's okay. I have felt the same way. My suggestion is that you be open to the idea of trying it. It's this easy:

- Find a quiet, comfortable place to sit, either on the couch, on a chair, on the floor, or on a pillow for added comfort.

- Sit upright, cross-legged. You can close your eyes, or you can look down at a point on the ground about two feet in front of you.

- Begin by focusing on your breath, taking slow, deep breaths. Breathe in through the nose and out through the mouth. The most effective breathing causes your belly to expand instead of your chest.

- Now start pacing your breath; breathe in slowly for a count of three seconds (one one thousand, two one thousand, three one thousand), hold it in for another three counts, and then breathe out slowly for a final count of three. Feel your thoughts and emotions settling down as you focus on your breath.

- Be aware that, as you attempt to quiet your mind, thoughts will still come in to pay a visit. Acknowledge them and then let them go, always returning your focus to your breath.

- Allow yourself to be fully present in the moment. This is often referred to as *being*. Not thinking, not doing, just being. Continue to follow your breath, and imagine inhaling positive, loving, and peaceful energy while exhaling all your worries and stress. Enjoy the quiet. Enjoy the moment. Just breathe. Just be.

- If you find that you have a constant influx of thoughts, it may be helpful for you to focus on a single word, phrase, or mantra and repeat it over and over again to yourself as you inhale and exhale. For example, you might try something like this: (On the inhale) "I inhale confidence ..." (As you exhale) "I exhale fear ..." You can swap the word *confidence* for whatever you feel you need to bring more of into your life (love, faith, energy, etc.), and swap the word *fear* with whatever you feel you need to let go of (stress, worry, resentment, etc.).

Meditation is a gift you can give yourself every day. For many Miracle Morning practitioners, time spent meditating has become one of their favorite parts of the routine. It's a time to be at peace and to experience gratitude and freedom from day-to-day stressors and worries.

Think of daily meditation as a temporary vacation from your problems. Although your problems will still be there when you finish your daily meditation, you'll find that you're more centered and better equipped to solve them.

For many people, this is the one step that is the easiest to skip in order to get to the more active, tangible aspects of the S.A.V.E.R.S. Resist the temptation; whatever form your silence takes, make sure you don't overlook this step.

Remember—your form of silence is your own. You get to decide. Personally, I do my silence in bed so I don't disturb my wife, who will often wake up when I do. (Be forewarned—doing the silence piece in bed is an advanced move, especially if you're prone to dozing while lying in the dark with the lights off. If you struggle to wake up, stick closely to the original five steps of chapter 2.) I lie in bed and try to foster gratitude each morning—to create a space of thankfulness for what I have. I truly believe that gratitude is an essential building block for an amazing life. Gratitude opens up so much space for you to accomplish more and leaves little room for less-productive emotions.

As I lie there in the first moments of the morning, I close my eyes and acknowledge my good fortune for my children, for the health of myself and my family, and for my great partners in business and life. Each plays a critical part in building wealth and a life of value, and I am grateful for it all.

A is for Affirmations

Have you ever wondered how some people seem to be good at everything they do and can consistently achieve at a level you can't imagine reaching? Or why others seem to do the opposite, dropping every ball, missing every opportunity?

Time and time again, it is a person's mindset that has proven to be the driving factor in their results.

Mindset can be defined as the accumulation of beliefs, attitude, and emotional intelligence. In her bestselling book, *Mindset: The New Psychology of Success*, Carol Dweck, PhD, states: "For twenty years, my research has shown that the view you adopt of yourself profoundly affects the way you lead your life."

Mindset is a critical part of wealth creation. It shows up undeniably in your language, your confidence, and your demeanor. Your mindset affects *everything*. Show me someone with a successful mindset, and I'll show you a millionaire in the making.

I know firsthand, though, how difficult it can be to maintain the right mindset—the confidence, enthusiasm, and motivation—during the roller coaster ride that comes with becoming a millionaire. To a great degree, that's because our mindset is largely something we adopt without conscious thought. At a subconscious level, we have been programmed to think, believe, act, and talk to ourselves a certain way.

That programming comes from many influences, including what others have told us, what we tell ourselves, and our life experiences, both good and bad. It expresses itself in every area of our lives, including how we feel, think, and act with respect to money. And that means if we want better finances, we need better mental programming.

Affirmations are a tool for doing that. They enable you to become more intentional about your goals while also providing the encouragement and positive mindset necessary to achieve them. When you repeatedly tell yourself who you want to be, what you want to accomplish, and how you are going to achieve it, your subconscious mind will shift your beliefs and behavior. Once you believe and act in new ways, you will begin to manifest your affirmations into reality.

Science has proven that affirmations—when done correctly—are one of the most effective tools for quickly becoming the person you need to be to achieve everything you want in your life. And yet, affirmations also get a bad rap. Many people have tried them only to be disappointed. There is, however, a way to leverage affirmations in a way that will absolutely produce results for you.

Why the Old Way of Doing Affirmations Does Not Work

For decades, countless so-called experts and gurus have taught affirmations in ways that have proven to be ineffective and set people up for failure. Here are two of the most common problems with affirmations.

Problem #1: Lying to Yourself Doesn't Work

"I am a millionaire." Really?

"I have 7 percent body fat." Do you?

"I have achieved all of my goals this year." Have you?

Creating affirmations as if you've already become or achieved something may be the single biggest cause of affirmations not being effective for most people.

With this technique, every time you recite the affirmation that isn't rooted in truth, your subconscious will resist it. As an intelligent human being who isn't delusional, lying to yourself repeatedly will never be the optimum strategy. The truth will always prevail.

Problem #2: Passive Language Doesn't Produce Results

Many affirmations have been designed to make you feel good by creating an empty promise of something you desire. For example, here is a popular money affirmation that's been perpetuated by many world-famous gurus:

I am a money magnet. Money flows to me effortlessly and in abundance.

This type of affirmation might make you feel good in the moment by giving you a false sense of relief from your financial worries, but it won't generate any income. People who sit back and wait for money to magically show up don't become millionaires.

To generate the kind of abundance you want (or any result you desire, for that matter), you've actually got to do something. Your actions must be in alignment with your desired results, and your affirmations must articulate and affirm both.

Four Steps to Create Miracle Morning Affirmations (That Produce Results)

Here are simple steps to create and implement results-oriented Miracle Morning affirmations that will program your conscious and subconscious mind, while redirecting your conscious mind to upgrade your behavior so that you can begin to produce results and take your levels of personal and professional success beyond what you've ever experienced before.

Step One: Identify the Ideal Result You Are Committed to and Why

Notice I'm not starting with what you want. Everyone wants things, but we don't get what we want: we get what we're committed to. You want to be a millionaire? Who doesn't? Join the non-exclusive club. But if you're 100 percent committed to becoming a millionaire by clarifying and executing the necessary actions until the result is achieved? Now we're talking.

Action: Start by writing down a specific, extraordinary result or outcome—one that challenges you, would significantly improve your life, and that you are ready to commit to creating—even if you're not yet sure how you will do it. Then reinforce your commitment by including your why, the compelling reason you're willing to stay committed.

Examples:

I am 100 percent committed to being as healthy as I can be so that I have the energy to be fully present in my business and with those around me.

Or …

I am committed to doubling my income in the next twelve months, from $_____ to $_____, so that I can provide financial security for my family.

Step Two: Name the Necessary Actions You Are Committed to Taking and When

Writing an affirmation that merely affirms what you want without affirming what you are committed to doing is one step above pointless. It can also be counterproductive, tricking your subconscious mind into thinking that the result will happen automatically, without effort.

Action: Clarify the (specific) action, activity, or habit that is required for you to achieve your ideal outcome, and clearly state when and how often you will execute the necessary action.

Examples:

To ensure that I am as healthy as I can be, I am 100 percent committed to going to the gym five days per week and running on the treadmill for a minimum of twenty minutes each day from 6:00 a.m. to 7:00 a.m.

Or …

To guarantee that I double my income, I am committed to doubling my daily prospecting calls from twenty to forty calls per day, five days a week, from 8:00 a.m. to 9:00 a.m., no matter what.

The more specific your actions are, the better. Be sure to include frequency (how often), quantity (how many), and precise time frames (when you will begin and end your activities).

Step Three: Recite Your Affirmations Every Morning (with Emotion)

Remember, your Miracle Morning affirmations aren't designed merely to make you feel good. These written statements are strategically engineered to program your subconscious mind with the beliefs and mindset you need to achieve your desired outcomes while directing your conscious mind to keep you focused on your highest priorities and taking the actions that will get you there.

For your affirmations to be effective, however, it is important that you tap into your emotions while reciting them. Mindlessly repeating an affirmation without intentionally feeling its truth will have minimal impact for you. You must take responsibility for generating authentic emotions, such as excitement and determination, and powerfully infusing those emotions in every affirmation you recite.

You must affirm who you need to be to do the things you need to do so that you can have the results that you want. I'll say this again: it isn't magic; this strategy works when you connect with the person you need to become on the way to achieving your goals. It's who you are that attracts your results more than any other activity.

Action: Schedule time each day to read your affirmations during your Miracle Morning to both program your subconscious and focus your conscious mind on what's most important to you and what you are committed to doing to make it your reality. That's right, you must read them daily. Reading your affirmations occasionally is as effective as an occasional workout. You'll start seeing results only when you've made them a part of your daily routine.

A great place to read affirmations is in the shower. If you laminate them and leave them there, then they will be in front of you every day. Put them anywhere you can to remind you: under your car's sun visor, taped to your mirror. The more you see them, the more the subconscious mind can connect with them to change your thinking and your actions. You can even write them directly on a mirror with dry erase markers.

Step Four: Constantly Update and Evolve Your Affirmations

As you continue to grow, improve, and evolve, so should your affirmations. When you come up with a new goal, dream, or any extraordinary result you want to create for your life, add it to your affirmations.

Personally, I have affirmations for every single significant area of my life (finances, health, happiness, relationships, parenting, etc.), and I continually update them as I learn more. I am always on the lookout for quotes, strategies, and philosophies that I can add to improve my mindset. Any time you come across an empowering quote or philosophy and think to yourself, "Wow, that is an area where I could make a huge improvement," add it to your affirmations.

I have a few regular catchphrases and affirmations. My favorites are the ones that affirm the day ahead. I like heading into my day with optimism. To that end, I use simple affirmations like:

Today is going to be a great day.

Things are going to move my way today

I'm going to be an instrument of good and receive good outcomes.

Remember, your affirmations should be tailored to you and phrased in the first person. They must be specific in order to work in your subconscious.

In summary, your new affirmations articulate the extraordinary results you are committed to creating and why they are critically important to you. Most importantly, they articulate which necessary actions you are committed to taking and when to ensure that you attain and sustain the extraordinary levels of success you want (and deserve) for your life.

Affirmations to Become a Level 10 Wealth-Maker

In addition to the formula to create your affirmations, I have included this list of sample affirmations, which may help spark your creativity. Feel free to include any of these that resonate with you.

- I am as worthy, deserving, and capable of achieving wealth as any other person on earth, and I will prove that today with my actions.

- Where I am is a result of who I was, but where I go depends entirely on who I choose to be, starting today.

- I am fully committed to dedicating thirty to sixty minutes each day to my Miracle Morning and the S.A.V.E.R.S. so that I can continue to become the person I need to be to create everything I want for my life.

- I focus on learning new things and improving my skills daily, and I commit to reading or re-reading at least one book to help that effort every month.

- I am committed to constant and never-ending improvement in the tasks necessary for my optimal day-to-day functioning.

- I commit to an "unplugged" period each week and month, in order to maintain my focus, mental and physical health, and perspective.

- I am committed to exercising for twenty minutes every day.

These are just a few examples of affirmations. You can use any that resonate with you, but ideally, you'll create your own using the four-step formula described in the previous pages. Anything you repeatedly say to yourself, with emotion, will be programmed into your subconscious mind, help you form new beliefs, and manifest itself through your actions.

The fact that it's possible to reprogram perceived limitations and create new behaviors is an exciting prospect. Your programming can change at any time. Why not start *now*?

V is for Visualization

Visualization has long been a well-known practice of world-class athletes. Olympic athletes and elite performers in many categories incorporate daily visualization as a critical part of optimizing their performance. What is less well known is that successful entrepreneurs and top financial achievers use it just as frequently.

When you visualize, you use your imagination to create a compelling picture of your future—one that provides you with heightened clarity and produces the motivation you need to make that vision a reality.

If you'd like some fascinating information about why visualization works, just Google "mirror neurons." A neuron is a cell that connects the brain and other parts of the body; a mirror neuron fires when we take action or observe someone else taking action. This is a relatively new area of study in neurology, but these cells seem to allow us to improve our abilities by watching other people perform them or by visualizing ourselves performing them. Some studies indicate that experienced weightlifters can increase muscle mass through visualization sessions, and mirror neurons get the credit for making this possible. In many ways, the brain can't tell the difference between a vivid visualization and an actual experience.

If you've been skeptical about the value of visualization, the science suggests you should keep an open mind!

What Do You Visualize?

Hal used visualization to reach a difficult goal that was well out of his comfort zone. He despised running, but he had made a commitment to himself (and publicly) to run a 52-mile ultra-marathon. Throughout the course of his five months of training, he used Miracle Morning visualization to see himself lacing up his running shoes and hitting the pavement—with a smile on his face and pep in his step. When it was time to train, he had already programmed the experience to be positive and enjoyable.

You can choose anything to visualize—a critical action step on your path to wealth, or a skill that you may not yet be performing at your best. You can even visualize actions that you habitually resist and procrastinate on, in a way that creates a compelling mental and emotional experience of the action. There are no constraints on what you can visualize, but there are ways to make your efforts deliver better results.

Three Simple Steps for Miracle Morning Visualization

Visualization meshes perfectly with affirmation—it's the natural next step in your morning routine. The perfect time to visualize yourself living in alignment with your affirmations is right after you read them. Here are the three steps that thousands of Miracle Morning practitioners follow.

Step One: Get Ready

Some people like to play instrumental music in the background during their visualization, such as classical or baroque (check out anything from the composer J. S. Bach). If you'd like to experiment with music, put it on with the volume relatively low. Personally, I find anything with words to be a distraction.

Now, sit up tall in a comfortable position. This can be on a chair, the couch, or the floor with a cushion. Breathe deeply. Close your eyes, clear your mind, and let go of any self-imposed limitations as you prepare yourself for the benefits of visualization.

Step Two: Visualize What You Really Want

Many people don't feel comfortable visualizing success and are subconsciously scared to succeed. Some people may experience resistance in this area. Some may even feel guilty that they will leave the other 95% behind when they become successful.

This famous quote from Marianne Williamson is a great reminder for anyone who feels mental or emotional obstacles when attempting to visualize: "Our deepest fear is not that we are inadequate. Our deepest fear is that we are powerful beyond measure. It is our light, not our darkness that most frightens us. We ask ourselves, 'Who am I to be brilliant, gorgeous, talented, fabulous?' Actually, who are you not to be? You are a child of God. Your playing small does not serve the world. There is nothing enlightened about shrinking so that other people won't feel insecure around you. We are all meant to shine, as children do. We were born to make manifest the glory of God that is within us. It's not just in some of us; it's in everyone. And as we let our own light shine, we unconsciously give other people permission to do the same. As we are liberated from our own fear, our presence automatically liberates others."

Consider that the greatest gift you can give to those you love—and those you lead—is to live to your full potential. What does that look like for you? What do you really want? Forget about logic, limits, and being practical. If you could reach any heights, personally and professionally, what would that look like?

See, feel, hear, touch, taste, and smell every detail of your vision. Involve all your senses to maximize effectiveness. The more vivid you make your vision, the more compelled you'll be to take the necessary actions to make it a reality.

Step Three: Visualize Yourself Taking (and Enjoying) the Necessary Actions

Once you've created a clear mental picture of what you want, begin to see yourself doing precisely what you need to do to achieve your vision, with supreme confidence and enjoying every step of the process. See yourself engaged in the actions you'll need to take (exercising, writing, selling, presenting, public speaking, making calls, sending emails, etc.). Picture yourself with a look and feeling of supreme confidence as you pitch that venture capital firm to secure funding. See and feel yourself smiling as you're running on that treadmill, filled with a sense of pride for your self-discipline to follow through. In other words, visualize yourself doing what you must do and thoroughly enjoying the process, especially if it's a process you don't naturally enjoy. Imagine what it would look and feel like if you did enjoy it.

Picture the look of determination on your face as you confidently and consistently grow your business, close more sales, or make effective investment decisions. Visualize your colleagues, employees, customers, and partners responding to your positive demeanor and optimistic outlook.

Seeing yourself as the person who has it all together is the first step in getting it all together.

Final Thoughts on Visualization

When you combine reading your affirmations every morning with daily visualization, you'll turbocharge the programming of your subconscious mind for success through peak performance. When you visualize daily, you align your thoughts, feelings, and behaviors with your vision. This makes it easier to maintain the motivation you need to continue taking action. Visualization can be a powerful aid in overcoming self-limiting beliefs, as well as self-limiting habits such as procrastination, and getting you to more easily engage in the actions which are necessary to achieve extraordinary results.

In "Lesson 2: You, Millionaire," we'll dig further into visualization when you create your Millionaire Vision, using the very same approach I still use to this day.

E is for Exercise

Exercise should be a staple of your Miracle Morning. Even a few minutes of exercise each day significantly enhances your health, improves your self-confidence and emotional well-being, and enables you to think better and concentrate longer. You'll also notice how quickly your energy increases with daily exercise.

Personal development experts and self-made multi-millionaire entrepreneurs Eben Pagan and Tony Robbins both agree that the number one key to success is to start every morning with a personal success ritual. Included in both of their success rituals is some type of morning exercise. Eben articulates the importance of morning exercise: "Every morning, you've got to get your heart rate up and get your blood flowing and fill your lungs with oxygen." He continued, "Don't just exercise at the end of the day, or at the middle of the day. And even if you do like to exercise at those times, always incorporate at least 10 to 20 minutes of jumping jacks or some sort of aerobic exercise in the morning." Hey, if it works for Eben and Tony, it will work for you and me.

Lest you think you must engage in triathlon or marathon training, think again. A modest amount of activity, especially if you're not currently active, can be a game changer. If you're already active, your morning exercise doesn't need to replace your current afternoon or evening regimen; you can still hit the gym at the usual time. However, the benefits from adding as little as five minutes of morning exercise are undeniable, including improved blood pressure and blood sugar levels and decreased risk of all kinds of scary things like heart disease, osteoporosis, cancer, and diabetes. Maybe most importantly, a little exercise in the morning will naturally increase your energy levels for the rest of the day to help you keep up with your demanding schedule.

You can go for a walk or run, follow a yoga video on YouTube, or find a Life S.A.V.E.R.S. buddy and play some early-morning racquetball. There's also an excellent app called 7-Minute Workout that gives you a full-body workout in—you guessed it—seven minutes. The choice is yours; pick one activity and do it.

Becoming wealthy isn't a sedentary pursuit. You need an endless reserve of energy to make the best of the challenges that come your way, and a daily morning exercise practice is the best way to get it.

Exercise for Your Brain

Even if you don't care about your physical health, consider that exercise is also going to make you *smarter*. Dr. Steven Masley, a Florida physician and nutritionist with a health practice geared toward executives, explains how exercise creates a direct connection to your cognitive ability.

"If we're talking about brain performance, the best predictor of brain speed is aerobic capacity—how well you can run up a hill is very strongly correlated with brain speed and cognitive shifting ability," Masley said.

Masley has designed a corporate wellness program based on the work he's done with more than 1,000 patients. "The average person going into these programs will increase brain speed by 25–30 percent."

Hal chose yoga for his exercise activity and began practicing it shortly after he created the Miracle Morning. He's been doing it and loving it ever since. I normally do some dumbbell weight exercises and walk the dog. If I'm traveling, I'll settle for doing push-ups. I try to do 100—but not all at once!

Final Thoughts on Exercise

You likely already know that if you want to maintain good health and increase your energy, you need to exercise consistently. That's not news to anyone. But what also isn't news is how easy it is to make excuses. Two of the biggest are "I don't have time" and "I'm too tired." And those are just the first two on the list. There is no limit to the excuses you can think of. And the more creative you are, the more excuses you can find!

That's the beauty of incorporating exercise into your Miracle Morning—it happens before your day wears you out and before you have an entire day to come up with new excuses. Because it comes first, the Miracle Morning is a surefire way to avoid those excuses and make exercise a daily habit.

Legal disclaimer: Hopefully this goes without saying, but you should consult your doctor or physician before beginning any exercise regimen, especially if you are experiencing any physical pain, discomfort, disabilities, etc. You may need to modify or even refrain from an exercise routine to meet your individual needs.

R is for Reading

One of the fastest ways to achieve everything you want is to find successful people to be your role models. For every goal you have, there's a good chance an expert out there has already achieved the same thing or something similar. As Tony Robbins says, "Success leaves clues."

Fortunately, some of the best of the best have shared their stories in writing. And that means all those success blueprints are just waiting for anyone willing to invest the time in reading. Books are a limitless supply of help and mentorship right at your fingertips.

If you are already a reader, great! But if up until this point you've been part of the majority of our society content to clock in and out, putting forth minimal effort for moderate compensation, you have an incredible opportunity here.

Although reading doesn't directly produce results (at least not in the short term), there are many activities that can pull us in other, low-level and less-fruitful, directions. These benefit us far less in the long run than a consistent reading habit.

Want to start a business? Grow your sales? Hire the perfect person? Build wealth through real estate? Improve your mood? Become more effective, wealthy, wise, happy, efficient or just plain badass? You're in luck. There are books on all of those things.

Occasionally, I hear someone say, "I'm so busy that I don't have time to read." I get it. I used to have that belief as well. But now I think of what my mentor used to say: "The greatest minds in human history have spent years condensing the best of what they know into a few pages that can be purchased for a few dollars, read in a few hours, and shorten your learning curve by decades. But I get it … you're too busy." Ouch.

You have one, ten, or even twenty minutes every day to take in valuable content to enrich your life. Just use some of the strategies shared earlier in this book, spend five fewer minutes on Facebook before you start your day, or read while eating lunch to nourish your mind and body simultaneously.

Here are some books Hal and I suggest you start with, and once you've primed your reading pump, we bet you'll keep going and never stop!

- *Wealth Can't Wait by David Osborn & Paul Morris*
- *The Art of Exceptional Living by Jim Rohn*
- *The One Thing: The Surprisingly Simple Truth Behind Extraordinary Results* by Gary Keller and Jay Papasan
- *The 7 Habits of Highly Effective People: Powerful Lessons in Personal Change* by Stephen R. Covey
- *Mastery* by Robert Greene
- *The 4-Hour Workweek: Escape 9-5, Live Anywhere, and Join the New Rich* by Timothy Ferriss
- *Visionary Business: An Entrepreneur's Guide to Success* by Marc Allen
- *The Distracted Mind: Ancient Brains in a High-Tech World* by Adam Gazzaley and Larry D. Rosen
- *Creativity, Inc.: Overcoming the Unseen Forces That Stand in the Way of True Inspiration* by Ed Catmull and Amy Wallace
- *As a Man Thinketh*, by James Allen
- *Rich Dad's CASHFLOW Quadrant* by Robert T. Kyosaki

- *The Game of Life and How to Play It* by Florence Scovel Shinn
- *The Compound Effect* by Darren Hardy
- *Your Money and Your Brain* by Jason Zweig
- *Taking Life Head On: How to Love the Life You Have While You Create the Life of Your Dreams* by Hal Elrod
- *Think and Grow Rich* by Napoleon Hill
- *Vision to Reality: How Short Term Massive Action Equals Long Term Maximum Results* and *Business Dating: Applying Relationship Rules in Business for Ultimate Success* by Honorée Corder
- *Finding Your Element: How to Discover Your Talents and Passions and Transform Your Life* by Sir Ken Robinson and Lou Aronica
- *Spirit Led Instead: The Little Tool Book of Limitless Transformation* by Jenai Lane

Books are tools to transform your relationships, increase your self-confidence, improve your communication skills, learn how to become healthy, and enhance any other area of your life you can think of—all of which are part of your wealth-building toolkit. Head to your library or local bookstore—or do what we do and visit Amazon.com—and you'll find more books than you can possibly imagine on any area of your life you want to improve.

For a complete list of Hal's favorite personal development books—including those that have made the biggest impact on his success and happiness—check out the Recommended Reading list at TMMBook.com.

How Much Should You Read?

I recommend making a commitment to read a minimum of ten pages per day (although five is okay to start with if you read slowly or don't yet enjoy reading).

Ten pages may not seem like a lot, but let's do the math. Reading ten pages a day adds up to 3,650 pages per year, which stacks up to approximately eighteen 200-page books that will enable you to take yourself to the next level so that you can take your success to the next level. All in just ten to fifteen minutes of daily reading, or fifteen to thirty minutes if you read more slowly.

If you read eighteen personal and/or professional development books in the next twelve months, do you think you'll improve your mindset, gain more confidence, and learn proven strategies that will accelerate your success? Do you think you'll be a better, more capable version of who you are today? Do you think that will be reflected in your business results? Absolutely! Reading ten pages per day is not going to break you, but it will absolutely make you.

For me, the greatest boost to my reading has come from listening to audiobooks. I read print or digital books most mornings, but audiobooks let me add to that while walking, working out, or driving.

Final Thoughts on Reading

Begin with the end in mind—what do you hope to gain from the book? Take a moment to do this now by asking yourself what you want to gain from reading this one.

Books don't have to be read cover to cover, nor do they have to be finished. Remember that this is *your* reading time. Use the table of contents to make sure you are reading the parts you care about most and don't hesitate to put it down and move to another book if you aren't enjoying it. There is too much incredible information out there to spend any time on the mediocre.

Many Miracle Morning practitioners use their reading time to catch up on their religious texts, such as the Bible or the Torah.

Unless you're borrowing a book from the library or a friend, feel free to underline, circle, highlight, dog-ear, and take notes in the margins of the book. The process of marking books as you read allows you to come back at any time and recapture the key lessons, ideas, and benefits without needing to read the book again cover to cover. If you read on a digital reader, such as Kindle, Nook, or via iBooks, notes and highlighting are easily organized, so you can see them each time you flip through the book. Or, you can go directly to a list of your notes and highlights.

Summarize key ideas, insights, and memorable passages in a journal. You can build your own summary of your favorite books so you can revisit the key content anytime in just minutes.

Rereading good personal development books is an underused yet very effective strategy. Rarely can you read a book once and internalize all its value. Achieving mastery in any area requires repetition. I've read some books as many as three times and often refer to them throughout the year. Why not try it out with this book? Commit to rereading it as soon as you're finished to deepen your learning and give yourself more time to master your Miracle Morning.

Most importantly, quickly put what you read into practice by scheduling time to implement what you're reading, *while you're reading it*. Literally read with your schedule next to you, and schedule time blocks to put the content into action. Don't become a personal development junkie, who reads a lot but does very little. I've met many people who take pride in the number of books they read, like some badge of honor. I'd rather read and implement one good book than to read ten books and then do nothing other than start reading the eleventh book. While reading is a great way to gain knowledge, insights, and strategies, it is the implementation and practice of these new strategies that will advance your life and business.

S is for Scribing

Scribing is simply another word for writing. (Let's keep it real—Hal needed an "S" for the end of S.A.V.E.R.S. because a "W" wouldn't fit anywhere. Thanks, Thesaurus; we owe you one.)

The scribing element of your Miracle Morning enables you to write down what you're grateful for and document your insights, ideas, breakthroughs, realizations, successes, and lessons learned, as well as any areas of opportunity, personal growth, or improvement.

Most Miracle Morning practitioners scribe in a journal for five to ten minutes during their morning routine. By getting your thoughts out of your head and putting them in writing, you'll immediately gain heightened awareness, clarity, and valuable insights that you'd otherwise be oblivious to.

If you're like Hal used to be, you probably have at least a few half-used and barely touched journals and notebooks. It wasn't until he started his Miracle Morning practice that scribing quickly became one of his favorite daily habits. As Tony Robbins has said many times, "A life worth living is a life worth recording."

Writing will give you the daily benefits of consciously directing your thoughts, but what's even more powerful are the insights you'll gain from reviewing your journals, from cover to cover, afterwards—especially at the end of the year.

It is hard to put into words how overwhelmingly constructive the experience of going back and reviewing your journals can be. Michael Maher, *The Miracle Morning for Real Estate Agents* coauthor, is an avid practitioner of the Life S.A.V.E.R.S. Part of Michael's morning routine is to write down his appreciations and affirmations in what he calls his Blessings Book. Michael says it best:

> "What you appreciate … APPRECIATES. It is time to take our insatiable appetite for what we want and replace it with an insatiable appetite and gratitude for what we do have. Write your appreciations, be grateful and appreciative, and you will have more of those things you crave—better relationships, more material goods, more happiness."

While there are many worthwhile benefits of keeping a daily journal, here are a few more of my favorites. With daily scribing, you'll:

- Gain Clarity—Journaling will give you more clarity and understanding of your past and current circumstances and help you work through challenges you're facing while allowing you to brainstorm, prioritize, and plan your actions each day to optimize your future.

- Capture Ideas—You will be able to capture, organize and expand on your ideas and keep from losing the important ones you are saving for an opportune moment in the future.

- Review Lessons—Journaling provides a place to record, reference and review the lessons you've learned, both from your wins and any mistakes you make along the way.

- Acknowledge Your Progress—Going back and rereading your journal entries from a year—or even a week—ago and seeing how much progress you've made can be hugely beneficial. It is one of the most enjoyable, eye-opening, and confidence-inspiring experiences, and it can't be duplicated any other way.

- Improve Your Memory—People always think they will remember things, but if you've ever gone to the grocery store without a list, you know this is simply untrue. When we write something down, we are much more likely to remember it, and if we forget, we can always go back and read it again.

Effective Journaling

Here are three simple steps to get started with journaling or improve your current journaling process.

First: Choose a format. You'll want to decide up front if you prefer a traditional, physical journal or a digital journal (on your computer or an app for your phone or tablet). If you aren't sure, experiment with both and see which feels best.

Second: Get a journal. Almost anything can work, but when it comes to a physical journal, there is something to be said for an attractive, durable one that you enjoy looking at—after all, ideally, you're going to have it for the rest of your life. I like to buy nice leather journals with lines on the pages, but it's your journal, so choose what works best for you. Some people prefer journals without lines so they can draw or create mind maps. Others like to have one page for each day of the year that is predated to help them stay accountable.

Here are a few favorite physical journals from TMM Facebook Community:

- *The Five-Minute Journal* (FiveMinuteJournal.com) has become popular among top performers. It contains prompts for each day, such as "I am grateful for ..." and "What would make today great?" It takes five minutes or less and includes an evening option so you can review your day.

- *The Freedom Journal* (TheFreedomJournal.com) gives you a structured daily process that is focused on helping you with a single objective: Accomplish Your #1 Goal in 100 Days. Created by John Lee Dumas of Entrepreneur On Fire, it's designed specifically to help you set and accomplish one big goal at a time.

- *The Plan: Your Legendary Life Planner* was co-created by friends of ours and is a goal-setting and habit-tracking system and planner for people who are ready for life balance and are willing to be intentional about achieving level 10 mastery in all areas of life.

- *The Miracle Morning Journal* (MiracleMorningJournal.com) is formatted specifically to enhance and support your Miracle Morning, to keep you organized and accountable, and to track your S.A.V.E.R.S. each day. You can also download a free sample of *The Miracle Morning Journal* today at TMMbook.com to make sure it's right for you.

If you prefer to use a digital journal, many choices are available. Here are a few favorites:

- *The Five Minute Journal* (FiveMinuteJournal.com) also offers an iPhone app, which follows the same format as the physical version but allows you to upload photographs to your daily entries and also sends you helpful reminders to input your entries each morning and evening.

- *Day One* (DayOneApp.com) is a popular journaling app, and it's perfect if you don't want any structure or any limits on how much you can write. Day One offers a blank page for each daily entry, so if you like to write lengthy journal entries, this may be the app for you.

- *Penzu* (Penzu.com) is an online journal that doesn't require an iPhone, iPad, or Android device. All you need is a computer.

Again, it comes down to your preference and the features you want. If none of these digital options resonate with you, type "online journal" into Google, or simply type "journal" into the app store, and you'll get a variety of choices.

Third: Scribe daily. I keep two things in my journal: my thoughts and my goals. When I sit down in the morning to write, if my brain has been busy—and depending on what's going on in my life—I might write a lot or just a little. For me, this ends up being one or two pages and takes anywhere from five to thirty minutes, contingent on the day.

There are endless things you can write about—notes from the book you're reading, a list of things you're grateful for, and your top three to five priorities for the day are a good place to start. Write whatever makes you feel good and optimizes your day. Don't worry about grammar, spelling, or punctuation. Your journal is a place to let your imagination run wild; keep a muzzle on your inner critic, and don't edit—just scribe!

Customizing Your S.A.V.E.R.S.

I know that you might have days when you can't do the Miracle Morning practice all at once. Feel free to split up the Life S.A.V.E.R.S. in any way that works for you. I want to share a few ideas specifically geared toward customizing the Life S.A.V.E.R.S. based on your schedule and preferences. Your current morning routine might allow you to fit in only a six-, twenty-, or thirty-minute Miracle Morning, or you might choose to do a longer version on the weekends.

Here is an example of a common sixty-minute Miracle Morning schedule using the Life S.A.V.E.R.S.

Silence: 10 minutes

Affirmations: 5 minutes

Visualization: 5 minutes

Exercise: 10 minutes

Reading: 20 minutes

Scribing: 10 minutes

You can customize the sequence, too. For example, I put the kettle on right after my period of silence, and then I do my scribing. I like to read my goals after that, which is part of my reading routine, and then I read a few pages of a book. Then I'll exercise *after* those things.

Hal prefers to start with a period of peaceful, purposeful silence so that he can wake up slowly, clear his mind, and focus his energy and intentions.

The point is that this is *your* Miracle Morning. Feel free to experiment with different sequences to see which you like best. The best Miracle Morning is the one that you *do*!

Final Thoughts on the Life S.A.V.E.R.S.

Everything is difficult before it's easy. Every new experience is uncomfortable before it's comfortable. The more you practice the Life S.A.V.E.R.S., the more natural and normal each of them will feel. Hal's first time meditating was almost his last because his mind raced like a Ferrari, and his thoughts bounced around uncontrollably. Now, he loves meditation, and while he's still no master, he says he's decent at it.

Similarly, when I first started my Miracle Morning affirmations, I stole a few from *The Miracle Morning* and added a few that came to mind. Over time, as I encountered things that struck me as powerful, I added them to my affirmations and adjusted the ones I had. Now, my affirmations are personally very meaningful, and the daily act of using them is far more powerful.

I invite you to start practicing the Life S.A.V.E.R.S. now, so you can become familiar and comfortable with each of them and get a jump-start before you officially begin The 30-Day Miracle Morning Challenge in chapter 13.

The Six-Minute Miracle Morning

If your biggest concern is still finding time, don't worry: the Miracle Morning scales down to fit the time you have available. You can do the entire Miracle Morning—receiving the full benefits of all six S.A.V.E.R.S.—in only six minutes a day. While six minutes isn't what I'd recommend on a daily basis, for those days when you're pressed for time, a great shortcut is to do each of the S.A.V.E.R.S. for one minute each:

- Minute One (S): Close your eyes and enjoy a moment of peaceful, purposeful silence to clear your mind and get centered for your day.

- Minute Two (A): Read your most important affirmation to reinforce what result you want to accomplish, why it's important to you, which specific actions you must take, and most importantly—precisely when you will commit to taking those actions.

- Minute Three (V): Visualize yourself flawlessly executing the single most important action that you want to accomplish for the day.

- Minute Four (E): Stand up and perform 50-60 good old-fashioned jumping-jacks or drop and do as many push-ups and/or crunches as you can, to get your heart rate up and engage your physiology.

- Minute Five (R): Grab the book you're reading and read a page or a paragraph.

And finally...

- Minute Six (S): Grab your journal, and jot down one thing that you're grateful for, along with the single most important result for you to generate that day.

I'm sure you can see how, even in just six minutes, the S.A.V.E.R.S. will set you on the right path for the day—and you can always devote more time later when your schedule permits or the opportunity presents itself. Doing the six-minute practice is a great way to start a mini habit to build up your confidence or a way to elevate your mood and energy level, on those mornings when you're pressed for time.

Another mini habit you can try is to start with one of the Life S.A.V.E.R.S., and once you get used to waking up earlier, add more of them. Remember that the goal is to have some time to work on your personal goals and mindset, so if you are overwhelmed, it's not going to work for you. Remember: *the practice is more important than the duration.* Develop the habit, however brief, and allow yourself to grow the duration over time.

Personally, my Miracle Morning has grown into a daily ritual of renewal and inspiration that I absolutely love. Even an "abridged" version of a few minutes is so much better than missing it completely.

* * *

With the S.A.V.E.R.S., we've now given you the full toolbox for becoming a morning person—understanding the importance of mornings, how to wake up earlier, and what to do with your newfound morning time.

Now it's time to shift gears. In Section II, we move from how and why you should wake up early to identifying the key philosophies and practices that are critical on your path to becoming a millionaire.

☙

Morning Millionaires

I get up at 4:30 every morning to walk my three dogs and work out. Around 5:45 a.m. I make coffee for myself and my wife, using an 8-cup Bodum French press. This is the absolute best way to make coffee at home.

—Howard Schultz, Executive Chairman, Starbucks

PART II:

WHAT MAKES A MILLIONAIRE

Six Wealth Building Lessons for Millionaires in the Making

LESSON I: THE TWO DOORS:

THE CHOICE TO BECOME WEALTHY

Most of us have two lives. The life we live,
and the unlived life within us.
—STEVEN PRESSFIELD, author, *The War of Art*

Imagine for a moment that you're a contestant on a game show.

Having fought your way to the final round of competition, you now stand at the gateway to the Final Big Prize. The studio audience—the boisterous crowd that has cheered you on all the way—has fallen silent. It's just you, the host, and the final challenge.

The host takes the microphone.

"Welcome to the final round," he announces. "It's been a long battle, but you've made it all the way. Complete this last challenge, and you win the Final Big Prize: all of your debts erased, and a million dollars, tax-free!"

Wow, you think. *This is what I've dreamed of.*

"Win this round," the host says, with a final, dramatic flair, "and you'll be a *millionaire.*"

The crowd cheers wildly. Then the lights dim, and on stage, a curtain rises.

There, illuminated in the beam of spotlights, are *two doors.*

A ripple of excitement moves through the audience.

"Behind one of these doors," the host says, "is the Final Big Prize."

Great, you think. *Fifty-fifty odds. I can do this!*

You open your mouth to speak, but the host interrupts. "Wait!" he says. "There's more!"

You wonder, *How much more can there be?*

A drumroll begins.

"The winning door is," the host says with a flourish, "the one on the *left!*" Lights flash. Triumphant music blares. The audience goes wild!

"Um…" you say quietly, as the room finally settles. "Did you just *tell* me which door to choose?"

"Yes!" the host cries. "I did!"

"So…I just have to choose?"

"Exactly," he says. "If you want to be a millionaire, *you just have to choose.*"

It's about this point that you expect your alarm clock to go off and wake you from what was clearly a dream.

But as crazy as it may seem, that's the real choice facing you and everyone else, and it's also the same choice that every self-made millionaire has made. They, and you, were given a choice not dissimilar to that of our fictional game show. A choice that essentially boils down to this: *do you want to be wealthy or not?*

Because what's important at the start of your journey isn't what's behind the door. It's consciously making a *choice.*

Your Other Life: The Road Not (Yet) Taken

Most people live their lives on the wrong side of a significant gap that separates who they are from who they can *become*.

That gap is frequently painful. Deep inside, we know that we can accomplish more—that we can do more, be more, and have more. And what causes us pain isn't that we aren't wealthy, for example, but that we know we *could* be. It's that unrealized potential that keeps us dissatisfied.

That dissatisfaction leads us to spend too much time thinking about the actions we should be taking to create the results that we want, and not enough time *taking* those actions. More often than not, we know what we need to do. We just don't consistently *do what we know.*

In those cases, it's easy to think you're missing some secret. When you see others excel, it can seem like they've got it all figured out—that they must know something that you don't. Surely, they must have some secret hack, tool, or some unlimited source of willpower that they draw on that you'll never have.

It's not true.

In my experience with millionaires, the first difference between them and everyone else is that they've *actively chosen to be wealthy.* That's the first step in bridging the gap between your current financial reality and the one you imagine: to *choose.*

The "secret," if there is one, is that choosing doesn't mean what you think it does.

Choosing Versus Wanting

Recently, some friends came to me for advice. They'd been wanting to invest in real estate as a path to wealth and thought I might have some insight.

This is a path I know very well. I built my wealth primarily through real estate, eventually creating a business that did billions of dollars in sales each year.

Bit by bit, they'd saved $70,000 to get things started, and now they were about to kick off their quest for wealth by spending $35,000 on a seminar that was going to, as they described it, "teach them how to buy and flip properties."

Now, they were standing in my kitchen asking what I thought of the program.

I knew the question they were really asking was something very different. My friends had one thing in common with almost everyone on the planet: they *wanted* to be wealthy. They wanted to be millionaires. The question they were asking was, "How can I get wealthy without trying too hard?"

I think you can guess the answer.

My friends are lovely people. And they truly wanted to be wealthy. Unfortunately, they lacked the common element that defines almost every millionaire: *choosing* to be wealthy.

They're not alone. A lot of people who think they want to be millionaires really *don't*. "I am going to be wealthy" is a lot different from "I want to be wealthy." *Want* is about the result. It's dreaming and buying lottery tickets. It's getting ready over and over again, with no aiming and certainly no firing.

Choosing is about deciding, planning, and taking action. There are moments on the road to wealth when each one of those things will be difficult. There are tough decisions to make. Difficult plans to create. And many, many challenging actions to take.

But in each of those moments, you make a choice. Each morning, you can wake up and do the same thing you've always done, or you can make a choice to be wealthy. Each decision you make can be in the context of your choice to be wealthy, or it can be in the context of *wanting* to be.

Want is wishing, and nothing more. *Choosing* is the first step in taking action.

Wanting is why people blow their money on get-rich-quick schemes. My friends had saved $70,0000 and now wanted to give someone *half* of it to teach them how to buy and flip properties. Instead, they could have woken up a little earlier every day to read three good books on real estate (often for free or low-cost).

In the context of *wanting* wealth, paying too much for free information is nothing more than trying to find the easy way to get rich.

In the context of *choosing* wealth, giving half your capital to someone for what you can get for free or extremely low-cost is known as *losing 50 percent of your money.*

Wanting is why people with little experience decide to day-trade stocks. It's the easy way, they think. Wanting is slot machines and lottery tickets.

My friends didn't want to build wealth through real estate—at least not yet. They wanted someone to give them an easy way to become rich. They wanted someone to hand them the real estate "secret." Unfortunately, that was something I didn't have. It's not something *anyone* has.

What I could tell them, and what I'll tell you, is that wealth begins early in the day. Wealth starts in the morning when you wake up, and you choose, day after day, to deliberately focus some portion of your time, energy and resources to becoming wealthy.

It's not a secret or a life hack. It's not a special technology. Those are signs of *wanting* to be wealthy, not choosing it.

Choosing is something else entirely.

But what is choosing, exactly? After all, if, like our fictional game show, you're going to choose the millionaire door, you better know exactly what that means.

Choice 1: To Accumulate Wealth

There are a couple of important distinctions about the word *millionaire* that we need to clarify.

Contrary to what many people believe, *earning* a lot of money doesn't make you wealthy. It can certainly help, but even a salary of over a million dollars a year doesn't make you a millionaire. The tabloids are full of stories about athletes and stars who earned millions throughout their careers but ended up dead broke.

If you earn six figures a year but owe ten times that on your home and credit cards, and have no other assets, *you are not a millionaire.*

The only way to be a millionaire is to own over one million dollars in assets.

If you want to get specific, the number you're looking for is $1 million NIPR (Not Including Primary Residence). Since you'll always need somewhere to live, it's a smarter target to build a net worth that doesn't include your home.

What Millionaire Means for this Book

People become millionaires every day.

In fact, many middle-class people can get there by just saving and investing. If you want to become a millionaire passively, you can max out your 401K, live frugally, save and invest every dollar you can, and you'll eventually get there.

But this isn't a passive investment book. *The Miracle Morning* is about taking control. You don't have to get up early to max out your 401K—all you have to do is place a single phone call to your HR department or financial advisor. This is an active book, not a passive one.

This is a book about taking daily action. And that means, for our purposes, when we talk about choosing to be a millionaire, we're talking about:

- Starting, or growing, a business
- Investing in real estate or other forms of wealth leverage
- Keeping your job, and starting a side hustle that you can grow into a larger business

If you want to build wealth slowly, using traditional investment vehicles, that's excellent. Use your mornings for that. But for the purposes of this book, we're talking about going further.

The first choice in becoming a millionaire is *to choose to accumulate wealth.*

Choice 2: To Be Strategic

In chapter 2, we looked at a five-step process to help you wake up early. Thousands and thousands of people have used it to help defeat morning rationalization. The reason the process works is that it's a series of actions designed specifically for a purpose: to help you wake up sooner by increasing your motivation level. It's a contrast to setting the alarm and hoping for the best.

One is a wish. The other is a *choice.*

When you make a *choice* to be wealthy, you'll notice something happen. It may be slow and subtle at first, but over time, you'll begin to notice that *your decisions and actions are being made in the context of wealth accumulation.* Once you make the first decision—to accumulate—you start to see your actions through that lens. And that means you start to become much more strategic about your life and your money.

Consider this analogy. Pretend for a moment your goal isn't to be a millionaire, but to have a lean and healthy body. If you were committed to that goal—if you were choosing it, not just *wishing* for it—then the way you make decisions would have to change.

- When you went grocery shopping, your shopping list would have been made through the lens of choosing healthier foods.

- Given a choice between walking somewhere or driving, you'd plan to walk.

- Tomorrow morning, instead of sleeping in, you'd think, "No. The healthy choice would be to wake up and exercise."

If you were committed to your vision of a healthier you, you'd begin to see all the choices in your life differently. Likewise, when you *decide* to be a millionaire, you start to see things through that lens.

When you consider buying a home, you might choose one that has a rental apartment, so you can cut your costs and have more money to invest.

Given a choice between leasing a car you can barely afford or driving an older model, you'd decide based on what it means for your plan to become wealthy, not on what your neighbor drives.

In the mornings, instead of sleeping in, you'd think, "No. The wealthy choice would be to wake up and work on my plan to become a millionaire."

Just like choosing to be healthy requires you to see your life differently, when you choose to be a millionaire, you also need to be strategic. You need to see your life through a new lens, where the accumulation of wealth is now a priority.

Choice 3: To Leverage

Many people have a simplified version of wealth that looks like this: *if I just scrimp and save enough, and work hard enough, for long enough, I might eventually amass a million dollars.*

For those people, becoming a millionaire means looking at the balance of their savings account and seeing seven digits. That's it.

In reality, it's extremely difficult to become wealthy simply by setting aside money in your savings account. It's possible, with a high enough income, but that usually brings high living expenses along with it.

In reality, you have to put your resources to *work*. You have to invest your money, your time, and your energy in ways that *multiply* your efforts. Money in your savings account doesn't multiply (at least, not very quickly!). It just adds up. Working harder at your job doesn't multiply your income. It just adds to it. Working longer hours at your job doesn't multiply your time; it just adds up to more time spent away from home, family, and friends.

The wealthy decide to *multiply*. They decide to leverage what they have by investing, by hiring others, and by allocating their time in a way that makes the most of it.

There's a whole chapter dedicated to this idea ahead. For now, know that waking up tomorrow and following your Miracle Morning routine is one of the best possible ways to leverage your time. By reading this book, you have already started!

Choice 4: To Change

It's so commonly said that it's almost a cliché: *what got you here won't get you where you want to go.*

In this case, the cliché is true and worth digging into.

Your life right *now*—everything from your work and your health to your relationships and your finances—is the result of choices you've made in the past.

The job you have right now is a *choice* that you made at some point. And, whether you realize it or not, a choice you've made every day since. You can tell yourself that you *have* to do the work you do, but the truth is, you *don't*. It's a choice.

Are you carrying around ten or twenty pounds of lifestyle-related fat? That's the result of thousands of *choices* that you made over recent days, weeks, months and years.

How about your significant other, or your close friendships? They're all *choices*.

Your furniture, the food in your fridge, the car you drive. *They're all choices*. They are all, without exception, the results of your past behavior.

The same thing applies to wealth.

If you've never saved a dime, that's a choice. If you've saved 10 percent instead of 15 percent, that's a choice. The way you chose to invest, or not invest, year after year…all choices.

Look around you, and you realize that *everything in your present is a result of how you thought, decided and acted in the past.*

There's nothing esoteric or woo-woo about it. It's cause and effect. You believed, thought, and acted in ways in the past that created almost everything in your immediate future.

Which leads us here: if you are not wealthy in the *present*, it's mainly the result of thinking and action in the *past*.

If you would like to be wealthy in the *future*, you'll need to change the way you think and act—*now* and moving forward. As the saying goes, continuing to do the same thing and expecting different results is the definition of insanity.

I want to be clear that this isn't just lip service. If you had acted differently, day after day, for the past year, how would your life be different?

- Would you have the same body?
- Would you have the same work?
- Would you have the same *money?*

If you want to be a millionaire, the most important choice you'll ever make—and the one at the heart of the rest of this book—is the decision to *change*.

* * *

Change, of course, *ain't easy.* Ask anyone who's made a New Year's resolution about their success rate. In fact, I suspect you can probably look at your *own* success rate. I've made all kinds of grand plans for changes that didn't work out. But the ones where I made a *choice* were the ones that I succeeded at.

The four choices mentioned above don't happen once; they are choices you'll have to make daily. That's the price of wealth.

- You can't spend all your money, or earn very little, and expect to accumulate wealth.
- You can't expect to become wealthy by accumulating savings in a bank account.

- You can't expect to become wealthy by making decisions that don't take wealth building into account.
- You can't expect to become wealthy *without changing*.

Those won't always be easy choices. But *you can absolutely make them*. And you have the same ability to make those choices as anyone.

Why a Millionaire? (What Powers Ongoing Choice)

People say, "Money is the root of all evil."

People get it wrong.

I'm not being philosophical. I mean, they actually get the quote wrong. The quote they're trying to refer to is from the Bible—1 Timothy 6:10, to be exact—and it says, "The love of money is the root of all kinds of evil."

If you just love the money, if you just want the money, if you just want to be wealthy for the sake of wealth, it's not going to work out for you.

Sure, you can make a lot of money. And sure, you can enjoy it. But unless you bring something to the table besides a love of money, you're going to burn some critical bridges along the way. Bridges like your health and your relationships. And those are bridges you'll desperately wish you had in the end.

Which is all to say: there's no faster way to screw up than to chase money *without purpose*.

I've never chased the money. I like having the money, but I've done more for the challenge. More because it was there – like Everest. Like a mountain. The money is a nice by-product of a life of challenge, growth and doing something that keeps you jumping out of bed in the morning. Money is a tool, not an end. It's a means.

Can you be happy with more money? Certainly. Happiness involves choosing to live a full and interesting life, and part of that is economic. Provided you do it with *purpose* I believe a life of economic abundance is fuller than a life without it. But only if that economic abundance comes for the right reason.

The problem with *why*, of course, is that it's easy to lose track of. It's easy to forget the motivation that first drove us to lose a few pounds, or start a business, or ask that special someone out to dinner. And that's why you not only need a driving *purpose*, but you also need a framework to support it. In the same way that AA has meetings and Weight Watchers® has weigh-ins, you need a structure to support your ongoing choice to be wealthy.

That structure is your Miracle Morning.

Mornings are your touchstone with *why*. They are a daily opportunity to create space—space for dreams, goals, and optimism. Space to remember *why* you chose wealth, and what it means to you.

That's why mornings matter to millionaires. Because without them, they lose touch with why they ever wanted to become wealthy in the first place.

Which Door Do You Choose?

So here you are.

The stage is set. You stand facing two doors. You know what's behind each of them.

The audience awaits your decision.

All you have to do is *choose*.

What door will you pick?

☙

Morning Millionaires

STEVE JOBS reportedly looked in the mirror each morning and asked himself, "If today was the last day of my life, would I be happy with what I'm about to do today?"

If the answer was "no" too many days in a row, he knew something needed to change.

— 5 —

Lesson II: You, Millionaire:

REPLACING BLIND SPOTS WITH A VISION FOR THE FUTURE

*The first principle is that you must not fool yourself
and you are the easiest person to fool.*
-RICHARD P. FEYNMAN, theoretical physicist

Of course, if it were as easy as a simple choice, we'd all be millionaires.

But we're not. Not even close. And that's because, while choosing wealth is an essential step on the road to becoming wealthy, it's not the *only* one. And becoming a millionaire means taking all the steps, not just the first one.

I speak to more than my share of people who are struggling to transform their financial life. Those struggles are most often variations of:

"I want to earn more, but I don't know how."

"I'm working like crazy, but I'm not any wealthier."

"Some people seem to have a knack for wealth. I don't."

My guess is some of those may sound familiar to you. That's fine—they are indeed real challenges, and you're not alone. My response to all of them, however, is always the same: "Welcome to the box."

Welcome to the box is just a shortcut phrase for a bigger idea, one that—from my perspective, after years of building wealth—is perhaps the most important concept to grasp on the path to becoming a millionaire. The box explains why some people, even when they *choose* wealth, don't become wealthy. It explains why you can feel stuck at a certain income or net worth, and why working harder so rarely seems to translate directly into becoming wealthier.

Naturally, everyone wants to know what the box is.

To understand that, we have to talk about crustaceans.

Hermit Crabs and Millionaires

You've no doubt seen a hermit crab—they're crustaceans, in the same class with such perennial (and tasty) favorites as lobsters and shrimp.

Unlike other crustaceans, however, adult hermit crabs have adapted to live on land. They breathe moist air, not water. And unlike lobsters and the like, hermit crabs don't have their own hard shell.

Hermit crabs do have exoskeletons, but they're quite soft on the outside compared to their crustacean cousins, and that makes them easy prey. As a result, they've evolved to borrow *other* shells. When you see a hermit crab dragging itself around on the beach, it's in a shell that once belonged to another creature.

As hermit crabs grow, however, they have to find larger shells to accommodate them—like a goldfish in a bowl, they're limited by their environment. Yet, interestingly, not all hermit crabs are created equal. Some stick with a shell longer than others. Some hardly ever change shells, while others continue to change environments over time. Some, at a certain point, just never change again. They stay in the same shell for the rest of their lives.

Humans aren't so different. But rather than physical shells, we have "boxes"—mindsets, beliefs and habits that we adopt over time, then discard when we've outgrown them.

We tend to change "shells" or boxes a lot when we're young and growing—both physically and mentally. But that process often slows down considerably when we reach adulthood. As we grow up, we begin to do the same things, with the same people. We have the same routines, and, most critically of all, our beliefs and ways of thinking become more entrenched. Like the more tentative of hermit crabs, we come to inhabit a mental "shell," and then we tend to stick to it.

That tendency impacts everything in our life, from our career choices to our vacations and relationships. But it's especially relevant when it comes to building wealth.

What Got You Here

The box is the beliefs, experiences, thoughts, skills, and opportunities that form your reality. It's invisible, but you can see the effects of it all around you in the physical world.

That box you're in right now no doubt fits you fairly well. You've grown into it, and you're comfortable. Everything in your box delivers a reasonably predictable result. Your current home, your friends, your job or business, the car you drive—those things are all the result of thoughts, beliefs, and actions that you took in the *past*. They're the result of your box. Every action you've taken was filtered through the box and through the patterns of your brain that help you decide—for better or for worse—how to live your life.

But that applies just as readily to your income. The box you're operating in right now is the same box that led you to your current income, bank balance, and net worth. If you want that to change, you need a new box.

When a hermit crab wants or needs more space, they leave their old shell behind and move to a new one. But it's a dangerous period. The soft-shelled, "naked" hermit is exposed to the world. It's a risk. But for the crab, it's the risk you take if you want a nicer house.

Like the hermit crab, you can only grow so much by staying where you are. Every day the hermit crab doesn't change is a day that *nothing* changes. The same is true for you. You're limited by your current box. And, although it may be risky, you're going to have to expand your box if you want different results.

If you want a different life—a different reality—than the one you have, you need to change the beliefs you hold, the thoughts you think, and the actions you take. If you continue to live within the boundaries of your current box, you're going to continue to get the same results. Like the hermit crab, if you want a bigger shell, you're going to have to make a change.

Creating a Bigger Box

You never *escape* the box. You always see the world through the filter of your beliefs and past experiences. You're always being "fooled" a bit by your brain, never quite seeing reality—that's true of all of us. But what you can do is *expand* the box. And you can do that in two ways.

The first is to become aware of the biases—especially the ones that are relevant to money and wealth—that cloud your judgment, inhibit your thinking and keep you stuck. Biases are like blind spots in your brain. They're ways in which you don't always see things clearly, in which you're being fooled by your wiring.

The second way to expand your box is to envision a different life for yourself—to craft a vision of a different box, one in which you have more abundance. One in which you're a millionaire.

One in which, like the hermit crab, you've traded up to a new shell.

Old Box: Uncovering the Biases that Shape Your Financial World

One of the most important discoveries about human life in recent decades, I think, is that we don't see the world the way it is—we don't see "reality" so much as we see a brain-infused version of reality, one that's unique to us.

If that seems a little far-fetched, know that this isn't pseudo-science. Everything you think you know and believe has been created by your brain—we have the neuroscience to prove it. The color "red" is an interpretation of light by your brain. *Your* brain. Which means the red you see may not be the same red other people experience.

This "brain filter" that we see the world through distorts our view of reality. It makes us see things in a way that's unique to us and often has a way of leading us a little astray, *especially* when it comes to money.

Don't feel bad—we *all* have biases, without exception. By becoming aware of them, you can come to understand the boundaries of your current box and what might stop you from expanding it.

There are *many* biases. For our purposes on the road to wealth, here are few that are most relevant.

Loss Aversion

We are wired to dislike losses. No one likes losing, but we humans dislike losses so much that *we dislike losses more than we like winning!* Gaining $100 feels good; losing $100 feels a *lot* worse.

That makes us attached to things we already have, and it also means we're risk-averse when it comes to money. Building wealth always requires some risk. If you're too loss-averse, it's difficult to reach millionaire status quickly.

Sunk Cost Fallacy

Related to loss aversion, this flaw in our thinking makes us prone to continue to pour resources into things that we shouldn't. If you've ever said, "I've already invested this much, so I shouldn't stop now," you've fallen victim to the fallacy. Remember: sunk costs are gone. You can't un-spend them!

Status Quo Bias

This refers to our tendency to want things to stay the same. Like crabs who never change shells, we find comfort in the familiar. Change makes us uneasy, and we have a bias against it…but change we must.

Time Discounting

This refers to our tendency to value immediate rewards over ones in the future. When you've opted for eating the gallon of ice cream *now* and worrying about your health *later*, you've "discounted" the value of your future self. This shows up financially in the form of not being able to delay gratification—spending money *now* that we could invest for a greater return in the future.

Ostrich Effect

We all know this one: the tendency to hide from reality. If you've ever left a credit card statement unopened because you didn't want to face the amount owed or put off dealing with a business problem that you *know* is a problem, you've fallen victim to this one.

Other Box Filters

In addition to the recognized biases that psychologists and economists have uncovered, there are untold more "unofficial" biases—beliefs and patterns of thinking that you have based on your upbringing, your peers, your culture, etc.

Those include things like believing in "hard work" without any thought to whether you're working *smart* (more on this in chapter 7) or believing that "wealthy people are greedy" or "money is the root of all evil." Each of these can be detrimental to your future prosperity.

We all have beliefs around money—a money consciousness that impacts our ability to become wealthy. Your job is to uncover those beliefs and decide which ones stand in your way and which new ones you may need on your path to wealth.

The only way to shift these biases is to become aware of them. Only then can you catch yourself when you fall into them. It's something that takes practice, but that's what mornings are for!

An excellent resource for exploring the many ways in which your brain can shape your financial box is the book *Your Money and Your Brain* by Jason Zweig.

New Box: Creating Your Millionaire Vision

In *Wealth Can't Wait*, my co-author and I wrote of the difference between your "air game" and your "ground game."

Your ground game is your day-to-day, nose-to-the-grindstone efforts to get things done. When most people think of work, they're thinking of their ground game—the sales calls they make, the number of nails they hammer, the words they write, or the fires they put out. Ground game is earning your paycheck, grinding it out.

To be sure, your ground game is essential. You aren't going to become a millionaire sitting around. But because most people *only* know their ground game, they are often stuck there. Your ground game is inside the box.

Your air game is another thing entirely. It's your 50,000-foot, mountain-top, thousand-mile view of your life. Your air game includes your plans and tactics for becoming wealthy—it's a high-level perspective on your life which ensures that the efforts of your ground game are focused in the right place. You want your air game to be one that pushes you to expand your box.

You can't have one without the other. All air and no ground means you wish your life away—it's what happens when you don't choose the wealth door, but just *hope* to become a millionaire instead.

But all ground, no air, can be just as problematic. That's when you grind out every day, working harder and harder, only to discover that all of that work didn't add up to meaningful wealth, or worse, that it didn't add up to *anything*.

In the next chapter, we're going to look at setting millionaire-level goals and creating plans to help accomplish them. But goals, plans and wealth all fit in a broader context—the highest air game that's called your *life*. All of those things need to come together in a way that fits the life you want to have. You can choose wealth all you want, but you'll never make it or hang on to it if it doesn't serve your life.

To make sure you've made the right choice, and to make sure that the financial goals you set are going to fit, it's important to define what it is you want your life to look like. I call that my *vision,* and it's the highest viewpoint of my air game.

I set one-year goals in the back pages of my yearly journal. I carry that journal with me everywhere; it functions as my notepad, to-do list, and general thought collector. By the end of a year, it forms a sort of paper record of my thinking over the past twelve months.

None of that, however, works without my vision. Where my goals are usually created on a one-year framework, I have both five- and thirty-year visions for my *life*.

Those vision documents—the highest level of my air game—take a unique form. Here's the process I use.

A Letter from a Not-So-Mysterious Millionaire

Imagine receiving a letter from a successful millionaire, in which that person not only described what seems to you like the perfect life of abundance but also offered you guidance and encouragement on how to create it. That letter would be as invaluable as it would be fascinating.

That's exactly the technique I use to create my future vision, only the wealthy person in question is *me*. I write a letter to myself as if I am at some distant point in the future (often five or thirty years, for me). In that letter, it's my job to describe my life and how I reached it, as well as to offer any guidance and encouragement that I can to my younger self.

You can do the same thing—have the happy, healthy and wealthy *you* of the future write a letter. It may seem a little odd at first but writing to yourself *from* the future delivers different results than the act of imagining the future from your perspective in the present. Doing the former requires you put yourself *in the shoes of the person you will become*, as opposed to just imagining the circumstances of the future. It gets you away from wishing and into the feeling of actual wealth.

Here are my favorite strategies for writing a great letter, from the future wealthy you to the present you.

1. Visualize the future as if you are there.

To begin the process, you can use the visualization techniques from the S.A.V.E.R.S. as detailed in chapter 3 to imagine a bold future for yourself.

What is your life like? What are your surroundings? How is your business working? What has it grown to? How are your relationships, your health? Envision it all.

2. Create your vision without fear or doubt.

It costs you nothing to create a bold vision that inspires you.

Remember: you're writing about something that has *already happened*. There's no room for doubt.

3. Write in the present tense.

Describe life as it exists in the future, but as if you're in that moment. You're not saying, "I will have a big home and thriving business," you're writing as if those things exist in the *now* of your future self.

You can also offer comfort and advice. Sometimes, imagining your future self can be a shortcut to identifying the things holding you back in the present.

4. Align your vision with your emotions.

Don't put something in your vision unless you feel strongly about it. It's easy, when brainstorming without restriction, to get carried away with things that don't matter that much—private islands and twelve-car garages. There's nothing wrong with those things, but don't include them *unless you feel strongly about them.*

5. Don't worry about *how* your vision will come true.

One of the first things that will happen when you start to imagine a future substantially different from your present reality is that thoughts of *how* to create it will begin to creep in. Those thoughts will almost always inhibit your vision.

For example, in your vision of the future, you might say, "I'm writing to you from our vacation home in France, where we stay for three weeks every quarter." For a brief moment, you're excited—you've *always* wanted to live in France.

Then reality creeps in. *How can I possibly afford a home in France? And who would look after it when I'm not there? And besides, I can't take three weeks off every quarter. That's crazy!*

The next thing you know, you're rewriting the vision you're passionate about into something more *reasonable.*

Being reasonable is not what vision is about. Your vision is about the life you want, not *how* you're going to get it. Forget about *how* for the moment. You've got weeks and months and years of *how* ahead. Now is not the time to *imagine* the life you want, but to *climb inside it.*

Remember: it's the future, and you're a millionaire. What is your life like? What do you want to tell the non-millionaire you?

Thinking about the vision for your life as if there were no limitations creates the beginning of stepping outside of your box. You might not realize that vision immediately but considering it free from restrictions is the first step forward.

Returning to the Present

Once you've crafted your vision without worrying about how to create it, it's time to begin the early stages of getting more practical.

For this, you'll still need to stay at the 50,000-foot level. We're not down on the ground with goals and plans yet. Keep your head clear and your vision broad. But it's time to give some thought to where you can begin to apply your time, energy and skills in the *present* to the business of creating wealth.

In his book *Good to Great*, Jim Collins uses what he calls The Hedgehog Concept, which describes the intersection of three circles—a place where companies should focus their efforts if they want to be successful.

I use a similar concept for individuals, in which you examine three circles in your life to look for areas of overlap that represent where best to focus your wealth-building efforts.

The three circles are:

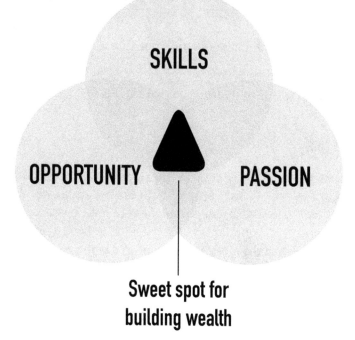

Skills

Having skill means becoming exceptional and continuing to improve. You can be in the most lucrative business or career in the world, but if you don't have the ability to do the work at a high level and continue to improve, you won't become wealthy.

Ask yourself:

- What am I great at?
- What do I have more experience than most people in?
- What abilities have I continued to improve over time?

Opportunity

Being exceptional in a business that creates something people don't want to pay for isn't going to make you a millionaire. Focusing your efforts on work that is in low demand, pays poorly, or has little future promise isn't going to make you wealthy. Becoming a millionaire requires that you focus on opportunities that have financial rewards.

Ask yourself:

- Is there anything unique about my situation?
- What is missing from the world that I can provide?
- What resources do I have, or have access to?

Passion

Passion shouldn't be confused with, "I have to love my work every second of every day." That's a trap, and it never leads to wealth. Yes, it's important to love what you do. You need to wake up excited about going to work. But your day isn't always going to be easy and joyful. That's a myth. Even the most successful people in the world, who *love* what they do, have hard days. They have to make hard decisions. They have setbacks and disasters big and small. They wake up doubtful. They question their choices.

Passion is about knowing you have the fuel for the journey—that you are inspired enough to work hard and continually improve. Without passion, you're unlikely to stick with it long enough to become wealthy.

Ask yourself:

- What do I enjoy?
- What things am I willing to do, even though they're hard?
- What things am I willing to do, even if I'm not immediately compensated?

The Center

There, at the center of the circle, is the sweet spot for building wealth. Even just *two* circles of overlap aren't enough—no passion means you run out of fuel for the journey, no opportunity means you go broke, and no skill means your business fails or your career stalls. You need something that touches on all three areas.

Millionaires operate at the center of the diagram, where the three areas overlap—that place where you do the things you're best at, where you are rewarded by the market, and where you continue each day because you enjoy your work.

The Quest for a New Shell

In a perfect world, you'd start your millionaire journey with a *tabula rasa*—a clean slate, where you had no past programming, no limiting beliefs, no scarcity mindset. In that state, you could envision the boldest of financial futures and push toward it with no fear, no uncertainty.

That, of course, is the case for *no one*. We all have a past. We all have biases and beliefs, fears and anxieties. There are no millionaires who haven't struggled with doubt—who don't *still* struggle with doubt. It comes with the territory—after all, changing shells may be risky business for us humble hermit crabs, but *that risk is what we are rewarded for.*

There is no cure for doubt and no box-free life. But know this: *mornings are moments of box-expanding freedom.* Your Miracle Morning is your time to think outside the box. To see beyond your limitations. To start over. To make a bold move and leave behind the safety of your old shell to strike out for something bigger, brighter, and better.

℃

Morning Millionaires

Five days a week, I read my goals before I go to sleep and when I wake up. There are 10 goals around health, family and business with expiration dates, and I update them every six months.

—Daymond John, American businessman, investor, author, motivational speaker and television personality

— 6 —

LESSON III: YOUR FLIGHT PLAN:

GOALS, PLANS, AND THE PATH TO WEALTH

Our ability to establish high-level goals is arguably
the pinnacle of human brain evolution.
-ADAM GAZZALEY & LARRY D. ROSEN,
The Distracted Mind

I f you could travel back in time to the earliest days of life on earth,
you'd discover that you share one thing in common with your
primitive ancestors: *goals*.

Even back in the primordial soup of our distant evolutionary
past—back before brains and nervous systems—single-celled
organisms were oriented toward goals. They had simple detectors that
allowed them to sense chemicals and move toward what was good for
them and away from what wasn't.

Over millennia, that basic goal-seeking behavior has been vastly
improved upon, but at our core, humans are still very much a seek-
and-avoid species. We survive through seeking out what allows us to
survive and avoiding what doesn't.

Surviving, however, is very different from *thriving*. Financial survival is something that almost everyone on the planet does well. People get by. They eat, they find shelter. They go to work, they get paid, they come home.

But making a living, as they say, isn't the same as making a *life*. Financially *thriving* means more than surviving. It means taking the basic pleasure/pain dichotomy of evolution up to a whole new level—a level you can reach when you harness your mornings to your advantage.

Goals and Plans

While we still seek pleasure and avoid pain, humans do have a lot of advanced brain functions at our disposal.

The first of these functions is that we can set goals for the *future*. Our complex brains allow us not only to imagine a future for ourselves as we did in the last chapter but also to set clear goals along the way that can help make that future a reality.

The second is that after we set goals for the future, we can create a plan to reach them. We can craft the steps, envision the obstacles, and identify the resources we need to reach a goal. Goals help you bring your vision to life. Plans help you reach your goals.

I call this combination your *flight plan*. It's a simple metaphor, but it works well. If you want to fly somewhere, you need two pieces of information in your plane: the destination (goal,) and the map (plan.) Both are essential. It's all well and fine to want to fly to New York. But if you've gathered your compass and your plane without a map, you'll be flying in random directions that won't get you anywhere close to the Big Apple.

You've probably experienced what it's like to have one piece without the other in your own life. Set a goal with no plan, and you get some short-lived excitement, but eventual disappointment when your goals don't materialize of their own accord. You get the "rush" of attending yet another seminar or setting another New Year's resolution but then drift back to business-as-usual.

Similarly, all planning and no goals leads to a whole lot of "busyness" that never seems to amount to anything. You're in motion, but your energy isn't directed—you're just drifting through your life.

As my wealth has grown, I've learned that one of the defining elements of millionaires is how purposeful they are. You don't meet many millionaires (and I have met many) who don't have both pieces of the flight plan. They know what their goals are and what their plan is to reach them. They know what they're doing that day, that week, that month, and they know where they're headed.

If you want your life to match the vision that you've created, you need to have the same purposeful approach— you need to have both a destination *and* a route. You need a flight plan.

In this chapter, we'll look at how to use your Miracle Morning to a) create goals that mean something to you, and b) build a plan to lead you to them.

Goals, the Millionaire Way

I keep two things in my journal: my thoughts and my goals.

My thoughts are what get *scribed* during my morning ritual—a collection of ideas, scribbles, brain-dumps, and other musings. It's an ongoing process, and not highly structured.

The back of my journal, however, is a different story. That's where I keep my goals. As a habitual goal-setter who's committed to my vision, I read my goals in the morning as part of my S.A.V.E.R.S. As I accomplish my goals, I put a highlighter line through them. I even use different colors to define my goals by category.

Lest you think I was a born goal-setter and type A list-maker, let me set the record straight. In school, I was a C student and a terrible procrastinator. If there was work to be done, I'd put it off as long as possible. (I hate to admit this, but I bought some CD's once that were supposed to contain subliminal "anti-procrastination" messages. I'm not sure if they worked—all I heard was ocean waves—but I know I continued to procrastinate for many, many years after.)

I'm not sure if there's a word for the opposite of setting and accomplishing goals, but I do know that I was the very definition of it for many years. If you struggle to define where you're headed, and you struggle even more to get there once you decide, *please* understand that you haven't been handed a life sentence for financial mediocrity.

After some fumbling around, however, it was clear that I'd indeed made a *choice* to be wealthy, but I hadn't found the path and the self-discipline. I was just slamming my foot on the accelerator and hoping to get somewhere, preferably earning a truckload of money along the way.

In my mid-twenties, when I began to get into business, I started to see that goals were helpful—it was great to have some sense of where I was headed. But once I wrote down a goal, it seemed destined to vanish into some sort of purgatory where I never looked at it again and, as a result, never thought about it much. As far as I could tell, goals went to wherever all those missing socks from the dryer went.

Since then, I've refined my goal-setting process to something that works extraordinarily well. Not only has it allowed me to transform from an extreme procrastinator into a goal-oriented achiever, but it's aligned what I do with many of the self-made millionaires of the world. To download the goal setting template I use, please visit www.thegoaltemplate.com/MM.

1. Set Goals in a Peak State

One of the biggest surprises on my journey to better goal-setting was that the goal itself was only part of the picture—what made an enormous difference was *the state in which I set the goal.*

If, for example, I set a goal when I was tired, overwhelmed or discouraged, I was far more likely to fail. Conversely, goals I set when I was feeling energized, optimistic and confident were ones that I was far more likely to stick to and accomplish.

The second state—the heightened one in which I was feeling at my best and most confident—is what psychologists call a *peak state.* It's a mindset in which you have increased awareness, mood, and energy. If you can capture and set goals in that state, you'll create goals that are far more inspiring and that resonate with you.

This is where mornings come in. The Miracle Morning is an ideal way to have more consistent and more powerful peak experiences before the day gradually draws you further and further into details and narrower thinking.

During your morning routine, watch for moments when you're touched, moved, or inspired. It may come during exercise, reading, scribing, or periods of silence. Any point in the S.A.V.E.R.S. is an opportunity for inspiration.

And when it comes? *Capture it.* Write it down in your journal—not just the goal, but also the context around it. What were you doing? Thinking? Feeling? What led you to think, "I want to do *that*"?

Of course, inspiration can arrive at any time, and you can try to create that state intentionally by watching inspiring movies, reading motivational books, or going to places that you find energizing. Your powerful emotional context could be a place in nature, a café, or at 40,000 feet high in an airplane. It might be found during a church service, as you spend time with friends, or while listening to a song.

Powerful states offer two advantages. The first is that you can set better goals. You'll choose things that energize you, and that you *want*.

The second advantage is that the state change is something you can return to when you review your goals, or when you hit an obstacle on your path.

- *Feeling discouraged?* You can visit that bridge overlooking the river where you first set your goal.

- *Procrastinating?* Go for that hike where you get your best ideas and solve tough problems.

- *Afraid of a next step?* Put on that song that triggers a state change for you.

The objective is to change your state to one in which you're touched, moved and inspired by something. To channel the mindset that opens your perception of what's possible and gives you the energy to keep going in the face of adversity. Peak states are fuel for your goals. They're a resource you draw on to become the *you* deep inside that wants more from life, including wealth—the *you* that wants a much bigger box than the one you're in.

2. Be Flexible

For years, I wanted to run a marathon. It's the classic of all physical goals—a test of mind and body and spirit. All the early morning training, dedication, pushing through "the wall"—running a marathon just seemed like something I should *do*.

I trained. I did those early morning runs. I squeezed in the treadmill time. And as a milestone on the marathon journey, I did what many people do: I signed up for a half-marathon.

It was awful. I felt terrible for days after that race. So terrible that I abandoned my marathon goal for the year.

And then I set the goal again. Along the way, I once more signed up for a half-marathon. Once again, I felt awful. I didn't like it—during or after the race.

I talked to a mentor of mine about the goal. He *loved* running, but he was plagued with knee and ankle problems. I didn't want those, either.

One morning, I looked at the goal and thought, *I don't love this. I don't want to do it.*

So, I took it off the list and never looked back.

The marathon, for me, was a *should* goal. I felt it was something I should do to prove to myself that I could. But I didn't want to do the work. I didn't want to run a marathon; I wanted to be someone who *had* run a marathon. I wanted the medal, but none of the work.

This is especially true of wealth goals. *Shoulds* are not great goal material. You're either going to do them, or you aren't. But they aren't the stuff of change, and they aren't going to accelerate your path to wealth. For that reason, you should be willing to reconsider them carefully and let them go as necessary.

Of the twenty-five to thirty goals I set in a year, I probably ditch about 10 percent of them. Some are small, some are large, but they all share one thing: they can be changed. Goals, for me, are living, breathing things. They change as you change. They can come and go.

Like milk, goals can have an expiration date. Sometimes, a goal only fits a certain period in your life and is either outgrown or needs to be put on hold. I love golf, for example. Normally, I play in tournaments, and I set goals for my performance. But this year I found I wasn't focused on it. I was starting a new company, and I was *very* inspired by that process. I found that while I was on the course, instead of focusing on my golf, I was thinking about work. I'd play great for eight to nine holes, then play terribly. The truth was, I wanted to work more than I wanted to golf. Golfing wasn't giving me the emotional fire. It had lost its context, at least temporarily. I had written on my goal list to take ten golf lessons with a pro to improve my game. I won't hit that goal this year, and that's okay because my inspiration is elsewhere.

I didn't just quit. It was a conscious choice, based on feedback. I knew I had to stop fighting the truth that I wasn't inspired by the goal, and I needed to make a conscious change.

While it's okay to let a goal go if it doesn't inspire or serve you, understand that economic success requires that you pick something that you stick to and find success in. We're going to dig into persistence and quitting in "Lesson 5: The Woodpecker Effect," but understand that while you need a certain amount of grit to become a millionaire, no goal is a life sentence.

3. Review Your Goals

It's shockingly easy to lose touch with your goals. You'd think that a goal that you set in a peak state, one that energized you and inspired you to take action, wouldn't need further reflection, but life has a way of bringing "goal decay" to even your most inspiring plans.

Your Miracle Morning is a perfect time to review your goals. It's the easiest time to find a peak state to touch base with the original inspiration that powered your goal, and it's often a time when we are at our most optimistic.

I don't review my big goals daily, but I like to touch base at least once a week with my flight plan. It's a chance to revisit my inspiration, check my direction and progress, and double-check that I'm still following a path that will lead me to the life I want.

4. Reward Yourself

Not every goal is its own inspiration. My 240 workouts a year don't inspire me, to be honest, but to get where I want to go, I know I have to look after my body. So I do them. For me, the workouts are gas in the tank.

Regardless of the goal, however, I find it helpful to include some R and R—some *reward* and *recharge*. That helps me to keep high levels of purposeful energy toward my plan.

Rewards are a critical way of closing the goal loop. You don't have to fly in a private jet to Bora Bora to reward yourself. You could drive to the nearest state park and make s'mores over a fire. But I do believe you need the rewards. Not just as a carrot to keep you moving, but as an acknowledgment that you've accomplished something. Simply moving forward and never rewarding yourself, for me, is a message to your subconscious that *all this work is for no real reason.* When you say you can't afford a vacation, consider that you might be telling your subconscious that *you don't need any more money because you're not going to take vacations anyway.*

Rewards also serve to help you *recharge.* If you treat your spirit and your body like a horse that you whip in order to work harder, the horse will eventually fail. The spirit will eventually die.

Treat your "horse" well. Feed it well. Take it on nice vacations if you can. Do that, and it'll perform for you in the race of life. (And don't forget the reverse is true: overfeed your horse and reward it for the wrong things, and it'll get fat and slow!)

I try to take a vacation once a quarter with my family. It doesn't have to be epic or expensive—you can hike in a national park for very little—but it's important to do. I've found that as a result of those breaks, I've become *more* productive and earned *more* money, not less.

Reward yourself with powerful experiences. Those experiences, in turn, give you new ideas, resources, capabilities, and an expanded sense of possibility.

Plans that Drive Wealth

Goals are destinations. They are where you want to arrive. They can change, and inspire, and be living documents, but they're still only where you want to *be*, not where you are.

To get *to* your goals, you're going to need a plan.

There are as many ways to plan as there are goals, and you should create yours the way that suits you. But here are the essential pieces of the planning puzzle that are most likely to lead you to success.

1. Always have a smallest next step.

Just as a map won't show you everything you'll encounter on a trip, plans don't include every step you'll need to take. But there is one step that's essential: the *next* one.

This is one of the best tricks I know of to keep moving forward with your plan. *Always* have the next step, no matter how ridiculously small it is. When I get stuck on a plan, it's almost always because the next step is unclear, or I have some fear about taking it. In either case, the problem can usually be solved by writing down the smallest possible next action.

Sometimes, that step is as simple as "ask a friend for advice." Sometimes it's to look up a phone number. But it never fails: make a small enough next step, and you'll find yourself moving into action mode.

2. Anticipate obstacles.

There are no perfect roads on the path to wealth. You *will* encounter problems, obstacles, and difficult decision points. With that in mind, you might as well be prepared for them.

It's easy to imagine obstacles like running out of cash or entering a recession. And while those are important to anticipate, remember that obstacles aren't always external. You'll want to put even more emphasis on *internal* obstacles.

- What habits might derail you?
- What fears might stop you cold?
- What skills, experience, or insight do you lack?

What are the most obvious problems you might face? For each, list the most likely internal and external obstacles, and then use part of your Miracle Morning to envision how you can overcome them.

3. Revisit the plan.

There's a saying that "no battle plan survives contact with the enemy"—in other words, plans tend to change once you get them out into the real world. That doesn't mean they aren't vitally important, but it does mean you need to consider them as a map where the roads tend to shift.

This is where mornings shine. As with your goals, mornings are the perfect time to revisit your plan with a clear and calm head. That's the time when you can review with the best perspective and the most creativity to adapt to change.

What Plans Look Like

Plans aren't goals, and they aren't just to-do lists. They're a road map of how you want to get from A to B—from where you are now to the life of abundance that you want to have.

Let's say, for example, that you're a realtor who wants to become a millionaire. What might your plan look like?

One plan, at the simplest level, could be this:

1. Become the best realtor I can be in order to maximize my commissions.

2. Save 30 percent of all commissions to create a fund for purchasing a rental property.

   • Buy an investment property.

   • Manage that property effectively.

   • Leverage that property to buy another.

   • Amass ten rental properties

   • Pay them off.

   • Be a millionaire!

This is a viable, repeatable plan to become a millionaire. It's been done by many people and can be done again.

What it doesn't include is every actionable item along the way. Every one of the previous steps is going to include multiple other tasks. And while you can't know all of them, you can know what the *next* one might be. For example:

1. Become the best realtor I can be in order to maximize my commissions. Next step: *Hire a coach.*

2. Save 30 percent of all commissions to create a fund for purchasing a rental property. Next step: *Open a separate bank account for my fund.*

3. Buy an investment property. Next step: *Set up an appointment with my bank to review financials and terms.*

4. Manage that property effectively. Next step: *Interview five rental property management companies.*

None of those steps are particularly daunting, but for our fictional realtor, they all might be essential. Every day, there will be new next steps, but the overall plan may remain more or less the same.

We could make a variation on that plan for a construction worker, a teacher or an accountant. All that changes are a few details. The construction worker might focus on fixer-uppers. The teacher might look for a property available in the spring, to be readied for rental while school is out when they can do the work themselves. The accountant might have access to alternative funding sources besides the bank.

The power of the plan isn't in knowing everything. It's in knowing the destination, the ideal route for you, and the next step to get there.

Now Versus the Future

Flight plans are fundamentally about the future. They guide your steps—they tell you where to go next and why, and where those next steps are supposed to take you. A good flight plan tells you where you're headed, how fast, and how to get there.

But it's important to remember that there is a *now*. That now is the life you're living, and it's wise to make time for it. I've seen far too many millionaires who denied themselves a *now* to the detriment of their relationships, their health, and their happiness.

One question I like to ask people is, "What's one thing you've always wanted to do with your life that you've put off?" I've heard many, many answers, including:

- "I want to visit Italy."
- "I want to return to the place my ancestors came from."
- "I want to get in shape."
- "I want to learn to cook."

I like to follow that by asking, "When are you going to do that?"

Again, there are many, many answers:

- "When I can afford it."
- "When I have more time."
- "When I retire."
- "When the kids are gone."

The most striking thing about those two questions? The answer to the first one is exciting and hopeful. The answer to the second is, in the long run, often tragic.

Goals are about the future. But don't make the mistake of putting off *everything* until some distant date when you have time, money and health. It's always possible that the time might never arrive.

Set goals. Create plans. Become your best self. Build the wealth you desire. But don't forget that you have a *now* that is also filled with promise.

❧

Morning Millionaires

OPRAH WINFREY starts her morning with twenty minutes of meditation, which she says fills her with "hope, a sense of contentment and deep joy."

Next, she hits the treadmill to get her heart-rate pumping. Winfrey swears that at least fifteen minutes of exercise improves her productivity and boosts energy levels.

Next, Winfrey "tunes herself in" by going for a walk, listening to music or preparing a nice meal. Finally, she always concludes her ritual by eating a healthy meal full of complex carbohydrates, fiber, and protein.

—Bryan Adams, Inc. Online

Lesson IV: Becoming Super:

THE POWER OF LEVERAGE TO CREATE WEALTH

It is not enough to be busy... So are the ants. T
he question is: what are we busy about?

-HENRY DAVID THOREAU

When I was in my early thirties, I woke up one day to discover a strange rash on my chest. Gazing into the mirror, it looked as if someone had rubbed poison ivy on me while I slept—there was an angry red stripe of pus-filled blisters sweeping across one side of my chest.

Unlike poison ivy, however, this rash *hurt*. It was incredibly painful. I had no idea what it was, but it hurt so much that I had trouble focusing at work, and off I went to the doctor.

The doctor took one look, sat back and said, "Shingles."

"Shingles?" I repeated.

"Yep. Shingles."

He explained that shingles was a recurrence of the same virus that causes chicken pox—something that, like many people, I'd had as a child.

"The strange thing is," he said, "you usually don't see this until after age fifty or sixty. You usually have to be older, or sick, or under a lot of stress. Frankly, I don't know why you have it."

I sure knew.

At the time, I was in Dallas running the real estate territory I'd purchased. I'd opened four franchises already, and I was going full speed, doing what I did best back then, which was *working hard.*

At the time, I thought working hard was the secret to everything— to wealth, to business, to success—and my strategy was to keep adding hours to my workday to get everything done.

And there was a *lot* to get done.

I was doing everything from buying office furniture and assembling cubicles to managing money, recruiting staff and repairing computers. If there was a job, I somehow had my fingers in it. But I was running myself into the ground in the process, and the painful case of shingles was my wake-up call. Here I was suffering from a condition that afflicted people decades older than me, or patients suffering from things like cancer or HIV. Clearly, something needed to change.

The ABC's of Wealth

At about the same time as I was being plagued by shingles, I attended a seminar and met a man whose net worth was almost a billion dollars. As we spoke, I did some quick mental math. I knew how hard I was working to generate a small fraction of his wealth, and I tried to imagine the work needed to generate a *billion* dollars. How could I ever get that much done? And how come *he* didn't have shingles?

I asked him, "How is it even possible to get everything done? My business is tiny compared to yours, and I'm falling further behind every day."

"The secret to my success is easy," he told me. "Each morning I write down the top seven things I have to do that day."

Top seven things, I thought. *Okay.*

"And then," he continued, "I do the first three."

"That's it?"

"That's it," he said. "That's my whole secret to success."

I watched him walk away, content, while I rubbed the fading scabs of my shingles.

I returned to the office a changed man. Where before I just attacked my to-do list in the order I wrote it down, now I began to assign priorities to everything. I gave everything an A, B or C priority. A's were top priority, C's were bottom.

And then?

I just did the A's.

Even if they were the hardest thing, or I didn't want to do them, I did the A's. The A's, I knew, were the most important things in my business. If that's what the billionaire was doing, then that's what *I* was going to do. End of story.

It was a revelation. Two things happened almost immediately.

First—and most surprisingly—I started having a lot more fun. Before, I was waking up to a day of endless tasks, most of which just seemed to be getting in the way of what I wanted to do. Now, I began to look forward to the day because I knew my time was being spent in the most valuable way possible.

Second, I started getting *much* better results. Things began to *happen*. By focusing my time on the most important things, I was able to accomplish far more. If I spent the day fixing computers and assembling cubicles, my business didn't grow at all. In fact, it shrunk. But if I spent the *same* hours focused on A-list items like business development and recruiting, things changed dramatically for the better.

Beyond Prioritization

It would be easy to label what the billionaire taught me as "prioritization" or "time management." And, technically, those labels are true. Putting things in order from most important to least is the most basic of time management and productivity principles; you'd be hard-pressed to find a book or workshop on the subject that doesn't include some variation on it.

But "getting your priorities right" doesn't capture what actually happened. It doesn't explain why prioritization *works*. How was it that a simple change in the sequence of how I did things could transform my results so much?

What the billionaire revealed to me was something that every would-be wealth-builder must learn. Some learn it early and easily; others, like me, get shingles. But whenever and however you learn it, the lesson is the same: *to become wealthy, you need to learn to get more from the resources you have.*

To grasp that lesson, we have to go back more than two millennia, to the Greek mathematician and inventor Archimedes. He's reported to have said that given a long enough lever and a place to stand, he could move the entire Earth.

Archimedes was speaking about physical levers, but his principle of *leverage* applies much more broadly. It explains why, when I started prioritizing my time, I realized I was having a far greater impact on my business in the same number of hours, or less. I wasn't just using my time; I was *leveraging* it.

Leverage is about doing more with the same, or less, input. When you use a long lever to move something heavy, you can lift far more with the same force. When I used my time more purposefully, I was getting *more* done. I was applying my time at the highest levels of my business, which meant that time was doing *more*. Same input of time, greater output of results. And in the case of my business, greater output meant more sales and increasing wealth.

The Math of Millionaires

We all have resources that we put to work every day. Each of us has things like time, money, energy, and physical assets, and we can use those resources to create value and build wealth.

When you use your time to work, for example, you're exchanging that resource to earn income. When you deposit your money in a savings account, you're exchanging that resource for a (very) small amount of interest.

Millionaires have resources, too. They have time, money, energy and assets just like everyone, but they *see those things differently*.

The non-wealthy think:

- "If I keep adding to my savings account, maybe I'll increase my wealth."
- "If I just add more hours to my day, maybe I can get more done."
- "If I put in more time at work, maybe I can earn more."

Those things are all true, but *only to a limited extent*. Where most people see the world as additive—put more in, get a proportionate amount out—the wealthy see the world differently. They know that addition—adding more time to the day, or more money to an account—is just that: adding. Millionaires don't like adding. They like *multiplying*. They like *leverage*. They want their investments of time, energy, money and other assets to increase *exponentially*, not in a straight line.

My meeting with the billionaire had introduced me to the first form of leverage: multiplying my time. Where I had been adding more things to my workload until I finally buckled under the strain, he was strategically adding the *right* things so that his time delivered the greatest possible value. Each day, I tried to do more things, while he just did the three most important. Every day, for years, he was *multiplying* his efforts, while I was adding mine up. The math wasn't working in my favor.

Once I took his advice to heart, I realized I could compound my efforts by changing how I spent my time. My time suddenly became more valuable. I'd increased the impact of my time by multiplying instead of adding.

The journey from shingles to leverage wasn't easy, but it was powerful. As one person told me after I began my post-shingles transformation, "It's like you transformed from Clark Kent to Superman."

I'm still not perfect, of course. I'm no Superman. But when you discover the magic of leverage, it can sure feel that way.

Wealth is a Team Sport

Of course, you've probably already figured out the catch with this elegant prioritization plan: there were side-effects to doing nothing but A jobs.

It didn't take long before those little B's and C's began to pile up. My home became a disaster—I'd given up on C tasks like housework. My business was growing, but my personal finances were in chaos because I'd stopped paying my bills—not because I didn't have the money, but because paying bills wasn't an A task. It wasn't the best use of my time.

Which all seemed great until my electricity got cut off and my credit card late charges arrived. Or when the office turned into an unkept mess, and the computers broke down because I wasn't fixing them, slowing office work to a crawl.

That was when I realized I'd have to leverage more than just my own time. I'd reached the limit of how much I could leverage myself. I was going to need help.

First, I hired a bookkeeper. And then an assistant. I began to surround myself with people to take care of the tasks that weren't the best use of my time. I assembled a team and learned another form of leverage: the value in multiplying through *other* people, not just myself.

If you poll the ranks of self-made millionaires, you won't find many who built wealth alone. It's extremely rare. Technology has given us some remarkable tools for leverage that didn't exist a few decades ago, but for the most part, *significant wealth creation is a team sport*.

Multi-millionaires know that it's extremely difficult to generate millions of dollars' worth of value on your own—they know they need to build a team.

Don't be fooled into thinking that you need to rush out and start putting more people on the payroll. That might be a reality for you, but not everyone is following the same path to wealth.

Your team can take many forms. You may have infrequent contractors and consultants to do specific things. A small business owner might have sales agents paid on commission or vendors who supply products or materials. They might have a virtual assistant to book their travel and appointments. A real estate investor might have a network of trusted tradespeople to manage repairs at a rental property.

You don't have to build an army of full-time employees to increase your leverage, but you do need to build a team if you want your wealth to grow.

Why Leverage Matters

The average person thinks that *work* is the most important way to become wealthy.

They're partially right. Work is critical. You'll never find a millionaire who thinks you should just sit around and hope for wealth. If you choose wealth, you're also choosing to put time and energy— what you might call "work"—into making that choice a reality.

But here's the important distinction: *work is less important than leverage.*

How could it be any other way? After all, many, if not *most* people spend decades working. Most adults spend the bulk of their middle years putting in some variation on the forty-hour workweek. But only a fraction become millionaires. If work were the most important strategy for becoming wealthy, we'd *all* be rich.

But we're not. Not even close. The vast majority of us are broke or, at best, financially *okay*.

There must be another factor at work. That factor is leverage.

How you use your time, your money, your energy and your talents is what determines wealth.

It's worth repeating. *How you use your time, your money, your energy and your talents are what determines wealth.*

Not work.

Everyone is working. The difference is leverage. How you use your time, your money, your energy, and your talents *multiplies* your work efforts.

For example, a real estate agent can work selling homes for their entire career. Each sale *adds* to their wealth. They can build a life that way, and tuck cash away carefully for a modest retirement. The more clients they attract, the more listings they have, and over time they can sell more property and work more hours to earn more. At some point, however, they reach a cap in what they can accomplish.

Compare that to someone who *buys* real estate, and then rents it out. Each property represents a monthly income stream that requires very little ongoing effort. The person who builds a real estate income business *multiplies* their time and money, with no upper limit on what they can earn.

Same market sector, very different wealth prospects. And the difference lies in leverage. Likewise, the person who works *for* a business has little opportunity for leverage. The person who starts one, on the other hand, has no limits at all.

Learning: The Longest Lever of All

In hindsight, I often wonder if that case of shingles saved my life. If I had kept working harder and longer, I probably would have worked my way into an early grave, or at least destroyed my health and relationships along the way.

The more I began to learn about leverage, the more I began to see the world through that lens—like I was viewing the world with super, x-ray vision that allowed me to see through the surface world of adding, and into the deeper world of leverage and multiplication.

What I began to see is that there's a natural progression in how most people learn about leverage and begin to take advantage of it. In business, you often start out alone. It's just you doing all the work at first. As you get busier, you quickly realize that you have to leverage your time if you want to get everything done. Spending your time on things that don't deliver important results, like filing papers, and you're stuck in adding instead of multiplying. Worse still, you could be trapped in *subtracting*.

When you get busy enough, however, you realize you need help. You can't abandon the Bs and Cs, like I did, and expect the train to stay on the tracks. That's when you start to add other people. You leverage their time to get more done—and, ideally, get it done *better* than you could do it.

As your wealth begins to grow, you realize that money is like time and people—it's a resource that you can leverage, too. To be multiplied, money also needs to be put to work. It needs to be in motion.

The wealthy have learned this. They know that money in a savings account or a coffee tin or under the mattress isn't doing anything. They know that to multiply their wealth, they have to put time, people *and* money to work.

There is one form of leverage that cuts across all these forms of multiplication. It's what I call the "master lever," and it's accessible to you *right now*. You don't need to have employees to put to work, or cash to invest. All you need is something that we all have: *the ability to learn*.

Learning is the master multiplier. Everything you learn, you get to apply over and over again. It's like having a single dollar and getting to spend it time and time again. Learning is the golden goose of life—as long as you nurture it, it will continue to pay dividends.

This, in the end, is the true value of mornings. In that quiet period of stillness, when the world is asleep, and you're in complete control—that's when you can learn. That's when you nurture the golden goose and pull the longest lever of all.

That's when you find your superpower.

❦

Morning Millionaires

I work out for an hour on alternating days and jog to the office. At the office, I review the to-do list I made the night before. I figure out my priorities and do those first. The day has a way of running away from you, so this makes sure the most important tasks get done.

—Barbara Corcoran, founder of The Corcoran Group and investor on *Shark Tank*

— 8 —

LESSON V: THE WOODPECKER EFFECT:

WHEN TO GRIT AND WHEN TO QUIT

A woodpecker can tap twenty times on a thousand trees
and get nowhere but stay busy. Or he can tap twenty-
thousand times on one tree and get dinner.

-SETH GODIN, *The Dip*

There are many benefits to knowing a lot of millionaires. Some of them are things you might imagine—access to a valuable network, extensive experience, capital. But my favorite, hands down, is that I get to talk to them about *how they got to where they are.*

Being able to ask someone how they've accomplished what they've done is an extraordinary gift. It's a true advantage, and it's one that applies to more than just wealth. If you know a great parent, a person in great shape, or someone who's an extraordinary friend, *that is a gift*—one that you may not have unwrapped. That connection is a chance to find out how they've done it; if you want to find success in any area of your wealth, *look there first.* The people in your world who have accomplished something you want to achieve are a great resource. Don't pass them by.

When it comes to wealth, there is one question I love to ask the millionaires I meet: *What are the three things that most helped you become a millionaire?*

The answers are surprisingly diverse. Millionaires tell me things like:

- "I see opportunities."
- "I'm good at leveraging others."
- "I'm a financial wizard."
- "I'm a hell of a salesperson."

Or, when I catch them at vulnerable, open moments, they offer different, more personal, answers:

- "I was driven to be a role model for my kids."
- "My parents were broke, and I'm scared to death of being poor."
- "I'm a workaholic."
- "I just got lucky."

Some of those reasons are more positive than others. Some are probably more helpful than others. But, in each case, I believe they're an honest assessment of what that millionaire believes helped them most.

There are two aspects to understand about this. The first is that you don't have to copy someone else exactly. If someone tells you that the key to their success is financial savvy, that doesn't mean fiscal expertise is going to make or break your financial future. Your path is your own, your advantages are yours, and your life is unique. It's wise to study the path of others, but even wiser to know how to choose what's best for you.

The second consideration is a little more interesting. For all the hundreds of different answers I've received to my "millionaire question," there is one answer that *always* comes up: "I never gave up."

That answer comes in various forms. I hear responses ranging from "I stuck to it," to "I didn't know what else to do, so I just kept going," but I've found that at the heart of every millionaire story is a singular idea—one that I think matters more than almost all others. That idea is *persistence*.

The Woodpecker's Dilemma

Persistence isn't a new concept. At its core, it's the grit to keep going in the face of adversity. Everyone from new parents to marathon runners needs persistence. But when it comes to building wealth, persistence is a lot more nuanced than most people realize.

Every wealthy person I've met has had to stick with something, often through extremely trying times. No matter what path to wealth you choose, if the millionaires of the world are right, you're going to have to do the same. *Persistence is not optional.*

You can call it grit, or tenacity, or plain old not giving up, but the essence is the same: when the going gets tough, the tough keep going. Or as Churchill said, "If you find yourself going through hell, keep going."

The problem with this advice is twofold. First, *how exactly do you keep going?* After all, the reason we quit things is usually that they are *hard*. If it were easy to become wealthy, no one would quit, and we'd all be millionaires. The pithy advice to "hang in there" seems, well, a little lacking.

The second problem is that *sometimes quitting is the right thing to do*. In fact, while persistence isn't optional, I can tell you from studying the millionaires of the world that *quitting isn't optional either*. You can't run a money-losing business forever and expect to become wealthy. You can't get a negative or barely-measurable return on investment and expect to become a multi-millionaire. Sometimes, you have to quit.

This is what I call the *woodpecker's dilemma*. A woodpecker can tap in the same place for hours and find nothing, or he can find dinner and live to peck another day. The issue for the woodpecker is to know when to stick with the tree he's on, and when to give up and move to another.

In other words, should he *quit*, or double down on *grit*?

Wealth building is much the same; it often comes down to knowing which to choose, and when. Persistence is a requirement. But so is quitting. So how do you know when to do which? How, like the woodpecker, do you decide whether or not to switch trees?

Let's tackle the first problem first—when to call on *grit*—by dealing with the three biggest reasons people quit prematurely: *mistakes, fear,* and *inertia*. Then we'll look at how to know when to *quit* and move on to greener pastures—or better trees, as the case may be.

When NOT to Quit

Just as there is an infinite number of ways to become wealthy, there is an infinite number of reasons to quit. However, not all reasons to quit are *good* reasons. A lot of them—perhaps the majority of them—are bad. Those bad reasons fall into three categories.

Bad Reason to Quit #1: Mistakes

Around 2006, my business really began to accelerate. Real estate was booming, and I was picking up huge momentum. I'd gone from opening one office a year to *four*. It was crazy. Sales were skyrocketing.

When you get on a fast train like that, the volume of things to be done is incredible. You can't find—and hire—people fast enough. You're on a constant search for talent at all levels and tackling an endless list of things to do and problems to solve. At that pace, you have to make bigger and more frequent decisions with what feels like increasingly less time and less information.

And that almost always leads to mistakes.

In my case, the mistakes were hiring the wrong people and leasing bigger office spaces than we needed. When the market began to crash, I was stuck holding office space and staff we couldn't afford, with people in place who weren't capable of doing the job they were hired to do. I'd gone too far, too fast; almost as soon as I'd launched them, I had to close down two of the offices I'd just opened.

There's a lot of talk about "failing faster" in today's business ethos. And while there is a lot of truth in the sentiment, it completely overlooks *just how awful it can be to make mistakes.*

Closing those offices was extraordinarily painful for me. I had to break deals. I had to admit that I failed. I lost money. And, worst of all, I had to let good people go—people who were building their own lives based on the fact that I had given them a job. Now I was taking it away. Anyone who can make those kinds of mistakes and claim they don't hurt is either devoid of humanity or lying. Mistakes are, plain and simple, *hard.*

In hindsight, of course, I can look at those experiences with gratitude. They *did* teach me important lessons about getting into business with the right people and knowing how to exit a business. But at the time, they hurt, badly enough to make me question what I was doing.

And that's the danger of mistakes. Each one carries with it not just the pain of the error, but the risk that you might not learn from it, or that it might lead you to quit when you shouldn't. If you quit because of a mistake, not only do you miss the learning experience, but you don't get to gain from that experience in the future; by quitting, you simply...stop.

There's no way to avoid every mistake. But I have found that when the mistakes happen—and they will—I can use my Miracle Morning to visit the experience from a place of calm and perspective. That's when I'm best able to reflect on it and learn from it.

Generally, that takes the form of questions—a sort of mistake "post-mortem" where I dig into the experience during the scribing portion of my morning routine:

- Does this mistake mean I don't love this?
- Does it mean I'm not good at this?
- Does it mean my business or plan is wrong?
- What can I learn from this mistake?
- How can I avoid the same circumstances in the future?

- If the same situation presents itself, how can I recognize it?
- How can I avoid making the same decision?

Usually, by the end of answering some of these questions, I've come to the most important realization about mistakes: *they are not the same thing as fatal flaws.* Mistakes are lessons. They aren't reasons to quit, but reasons to *get better.* They are what will make you who you are, and I've never met a millionaire who hasn't made plenty of errors along the way.

Bad Reason to Quit #2: Fear

They say that the mind is a wonderful servant and a terrible master.

When you're in charge of your mind—when you're the master—you can accomplish incredible things. When your mind masters *you,* you allow yourself to give in to worry, anxiety, and fear, and they can be growth killers.

This has real consequences for building wealth. Long ago, when I was struggling at work, a friend told me, "You know, you're ready-aim...ready-aim...ready-aim. There's no fire with you."

He was right. I used to suffer from analysis paralysis. I would agonize over actions and decisions, worried that I might make a mistake (sound familiar?), or afraid that I'd be rejected or fail. His honesty helped me see that I had to break free from that fear in order to grow.

The solution, I discovered, was to *act immediately to do the thing you fear.*

For example, if the important thing you have to do today is hard or intimidating—say, a cold sales call, or speaking with an angry client that you've messed up with—the only way I've found to not freeze in the headlights is to *act* as quickly as possible. Once you start thinking, you become a servant to your mind, and then it's nearly impossible to think your way out. Don't think about it. Just *do* it.

When you ask yourself, "What's the best way to grow my business?" and the answer is, "Call that prospective high-end client," then just *do* it. Take action. Don't think. Feel the anxiety but take action anyway.

What you're developing is the skill of taking action in the face of fear and uncertainty—and believe me, it *is* a skill. It's a skill that your Miracle Morning is a perfect time for working on. A calm morning that you start on your terms, at your pace, in your control, is almost guaranteed to reduce your fear and anxiety. It's the time when you can think of that anxious or fearful voice in your head not as a truth-teller, but more like an annoying neighbor who keeps wandering into your mental yard. That neighbor used to distract me and lead me to thoughts of quitting. Now, nine times out of ten, I ignore him.

Don't confuse fear and anxiety with the value of what you're doing to increase your wealth. The fact that you feel fear doesn't mean you're on the wrong track. Anxiety doesn't mean your business will fail, or you'll fall into financial ruin. Sometimes, fear and anxiety are sure signs to push forward, not signs to quit.

Bad Reason to Quit #3: Inertia

The person who takes the most action in the face of fear—even if they're half wrong—will beat the person who never moves forward, every time. The person who never takes action will almost always quit for one critical reason: they lack momentum.

When you start doing the important, big, and scary things, you start to see results. Over time, you begin to build proof that bold action delivers results—financially and personally.

It's this "virtuous cycle" that explains why people who have made—and lost—millions often become millionaires again. They have the proof and the experience that bold, purposeful action delivers results. If they make a mistake, they start again knowing that eventually, they'll get it right.

Sometimes, especially for those building wealth for the first time, a series of mistakes or a lack of progress can start a negative cycle. The less progress you make, the more confidence you lose and the more you worry. The more you worry, the less action you take. Before you know it, you've ground to a halt.

If this speaks to you, know that you're not alone. Momentum and energy tend to ebb and flow with life. The secret is to minimize the ebbs, and don't take them as immediate signs that you should quit.

I use mornings as a tool to keep my momentum up by:

- **Reviewing goals.** Sometimes we lose momentum by losing touch with where we're going. It may sound simple, but you'd be surprised how easy it is to disconnect from your goals without realizing it. I use my morning ritual to review my goals once a week. For example, one of my goals is to exercise 240 times a year. Without touching base with my goals and checking my progress, I'd almost certainly lose track. Plus, when I check in, I get a reminder of what inspired me to set those goals in the first place.

- **Maintaining health and physical energy.** It's hard to keep your momentum up if you have no physical energy. Eat well every day. Move every day. Use your Miracle Morning routine to create momentum. Don't fall into the trap of thinking that waking up a little earlier will make you exhausted; your mornings are a tool to do just the opposite! Review the "Not-So-Obvious Principle #2: Energy Engineering" chapter for more ways to engineer your energy and rebuild momentum.

- **Managing my environment.** Energy doesn't just come from within. Perhaps nothing can affect your energy levels more than the people you surround yourself with. Your friends, mentors, employees, partners, colleagues, and customers— they all influence your energy levels, and that in turn can affect whether your momentum spirals virtuously up or negatively down. You need to treat your relationships like a garden, cultivating what you love and pruning what detracts from your life and momentum. If you need help, turn to the Miracle Morning Community. It's a great source of ongoing support, authentic help, and true momentum building. And when in doubt? Hug your loved ones. That's energy just waiting for you!

When to Quit

In 2006, I started a business and lost a million dollars.

The business was a English language school for recent immigrants. I thought it was a great idea, and a unique niche in the market; I was excited about it.

But there were a couple of problems. The first was that the timing, in hindsight, wasn't great—it was not long before the U.S. housing crash. No matter how well the business did, there was a good chance I would have found trouble ahead simply because the economy was going to tank.

The more immediate and relevant problem was that I'd hired the wrong person to manage the business. While I'd learned from my shingles experience that I couldn't do everything myself, I hadn't quite mastered the process of hiring the right people for certain jobs. In this case, I had the wrong one, and I didn't hold the person accountable enough; as a result, the business was spiraling downward.

Before I knew it, we were out of business, and I was a million dollars in the hole.

In this case, however, there was a deeper issue. The biggest mistake I'd made wasn't timing the market or hiring wrong. It was *failing to quit.*

We've been focusing so far on how *not* to quit—how to persist and stick with your plan to create wealth.

But the truth is, people quit things all the time as a necessary step toward wealth. It's unlikely that everything you do is something you'll stick with or that every plan is going to be the one that works. Sometimes, you have to cut your losses.

In my case, I had a chance to get out of the language school business sooner. After about $350,000 in losses, there came a point where it would have been "relatively" easy to walk away. Instead, I doubled down. I stuck with it and invested another $650,000. Not many months later, the writing was on the wall—or, more accurately, I was *reading* the writing that had been there all along—and I pulled the plug.

Money lost, painful lesson learned.

Or at least, I *hoped* the lesson was learned. I have given a lot of thought to that loss—and to others—in the years since, in an attempt to figure out why I didn't quit sooner and how I could learn to be a "better quitter."

An Algorithm for Quitting

In *Born for This: How to Find the Work You Were Meant to Do*, author Chris Guillebeau uses two simple questions to decide when to quit. It's a simple yet very powerful tool to help you decide when it's time to quit difficult, larger things like businesses, relationships, and jobs.

The two questions are:

1. Is it working?
2. Do you still enjoy it?

1. Is it working?

For our context, the "is it working" question is a financial one. This is, after all, a book about wealth. If the direction you're headed isn't going to help you become a millionaire, then it's time to quit.

Is the path you're on right now going to deliver the wealth you want, in the time you want? *That's* the question you need to ask. And if the answer is no, then it's time to either make a change or quit entirely.

But which option do you choose?

To find out, you'll need to ask the second question.

2. Do you still enjoy it?

There's more to life than money. Take it from someone who's spent much of his life creating wealth: *money can't be the only thing.*

And, per previous discussions in the "Lesson 2: You, Millionaire" chapter, there's also no easy way to separate finances from emotions; doing something you hate for a long time isn't a recipe for becoming a successful millionaire. That's where we have to bring something else into the equation: your enjoyment of the process.

Are you still enjoying the work? The business, the side hustle, the investment process? Whatever you're doing to create wealth, *are you enjoying it?*

If we plot your answers to both these questions, we get a quadrant that looks like this:

It's insightful. The first thing you'll notice is that *there's only one circumstance under which you should quit.* That's when something isn't working, *and* you don't like it. Otherwise, you should either stick to your plan and double down on grit, or you should make a change.

Let's go back to our rental property example. If you're losing money, then *it's not working.* But before you do anything, ask yourself, *am I still enjoying it?*

If the answer is no, then it may be time to reconsider. But if you like owning property, then there's a host of things you could consider before quitting. Can you remortgage to cut costs? Raise rents? Remodel to increase value or add more tenants?

The same goes for a business. A business that loses money in the short term may be able to be resuscitated. Ask yourself, "What is the best possible outcome? What is the most likely outcome? What is the worst possible outcome?". You don't want to quit something you love that can be fixed. But what if you don't like something, or it can't be fixed?

Then it's time to do what smart millionaires do and *quit*.

Remember, though, that just as you can quit for the wrong reasons, you can also stick with something for the wrong reasons. Your tenacity can work against you, too. Here are two of the most common reasons for not quitting when we should:

Sunk cost fallacy. Remember this one? Our brains are wired to dislike losses. In fact, we dislike losses more than we like winning. That makes us attached to things we already have (like a losing business or investment), and it makes us prone to continue to pour resources into things that we shouldn't—to stick when we should quit. Remember: sunk costs are gone. You can't un-spend them by adding more.

Fear. Just as fear can drive us to quit something we should stick with, the reverse is true, too. Fear of feeling like a failure, or fear of embarrassment, can make us stay with things much longer than we should. There's nothing wrong with fear; the game is to try to identify when fear is stopping you from making the best decision or taking the best action.

The Grit–Quit Tension

The game isn't—as the world would have you believe—to "never give up." Nor is it to "always cut your losses." The solution is more nuanced. It's a path of balancing persistence with quitting while you're ahead—a kind of "grit-quit" tension that you need to maintain in order to bring your plans to fruition.

To grit or to quit, that is the question—and it's where Miracle Mornings shine.

It's difficult to make a serious decision about whether you should stick to your plan when you're buried in the chaos of a busy day. You either won't be able to even consider the choice, or you won't be able to make a clear and considered decision.

Your Miracle Morning is the perfect opportunity to find the headspace you need. That's the time of day when you can look at the big picture and make a decision that takes into account everything that matters.

Persistence isn't optional for building wealth. You're going to have to stick to your plan through daunting obstacles and tough times.

But quitting isn't optional, either. There are times you're going to have to cut your losses.

Your job, if you want to become a millionaire, is to know the difference.

❧

Morning Millionaires

JACK DORSEY, CEO of both Twitter and Square, wakes at 5 a.m. to meditate for half an hour and do a workout before heading to his favorite coffee shop for breakfast. ☒

"Up at 5, meditate for 30, seven minute workout times three, make coffee, check in. I sleep from 11-5 a.m. usually. Blackout shades help. Meditation and exercise!"

— 9 —

LESSON VI: SHOW ME THE MONEY:

UNDERSTANDING WHAT MONEY MEASURES

"If we command our wealth, we shall be rich and free. If our wealth commands us, we are poor indeed."

-Edmund Burke

Show me the money.

That may be what you're wondering right now. And rightly so—we've managed to get eight chapters into a book about becoming a millionaire without talking much about money.

There's a good reason for this. Money, while technically the absolute measure of whether you've reached the goal of becoming a millionaire, is just that—a measure. It's a yardstick. Money is a way of keeping score, but as is so often the case, the score only tells you so much about how the game is played.

What we've been discussing instead are the things that are most critical in ensuring that you *have* something to measure—the things that put the score on the board. They are the essential lessons of wealth building:

- Actively *choosing* to accumulate wealth
- Defining a *vision* for your life that will inspire you to take action daily
- Creating a *flight plan* to guide your efforts
- Learning to multiply your time and energy through the power of *leverage*
- Developing the skill of knowing when to *grit*, and when to *quit*

There are few millionaires who haven't built capacity in all those areas. Each is crucial, and each plays its part on the road to wealth.

But, that being said, there are also no millionaires without *money*. With that in mind, it's time to get down to talking about you and your cash. In this chapter, we'll look at five money-specific concepts that every aspiring millionaire must understand and embrace.

Principle #1: Wealth Begins with Your Personal Finances

It's easy to think of millionaires in terms of grand lifestyles, big businesses, stock portfolios, or high-flying, C-suite executive positions. The truth, however, begins with something much humbler and closer to home. It begins with something we all have control over: our personal finances.

That may seem odd—after all, it's not like you're going to find a million dollars under your sofa cushions, or in a savings account you forgot about. But your personal finances *as they are today* are critical because they represent your habits and attitudes toward money.

For example, it's easy to think that a million dollars will make everything so much easier, but it's not that simple. Wherever you go, you take yourself with you; if you're spending 110% of what you earn now, then you'll be able to spend 110% of a few million as well. Trust me; it's easier than you might think.

In short, *if you can't manage what you have, you'll never make or keep more.* Make whatever adjustments you need to make to your lifestyle to be able to live off less than your current income.

What do you do with the difference? *Put it aside.* Building a surplus gives you options. You can invest. You can make better choices about work and business. You can operate with a clearer head. If you're running a deficit in your personal life, it's going to make change hard—and as you know by now, change is exactly what needs to happen.

This isn't a "save for the future" lecture like your parents might have given you. This is about learning to effectively manage what you have *now* so that you don't carry bad habits forward, and so that you have the headspace to make the kind of decisions that millionaires make, not the ones that everyone else does.

I recommend that you start by taking 10 percent of whatever funds you have in the bank right now and putting it into a separate savings account. Make it automatic, and keep it separate. The bigger that fund gets, the more options you have.

Remember, too, that most wealthy people give a percentage of their income to causes they believe in. But you don't have to wait until you're wealthy to start this practice. Tony Robbins said, "If you won't give $1 out of $10, you'll never give $1 million out of $10 million." If you can't do 10 percent without bouncing a rent check, then start with five. Or two. Or a simple one percent. It's not the amount that matters, but instead developing the mindset and creating a habit that will change your financial future and serve you for the rest of your life.

You've got to start teaching your subconscious brain that it can produce an abundant income. You need to believe that there's more than enough and that there is always more on the way.

If you can't manage what you have, you won't be able to effectively manage more.

Principle #2: Money Has Velocity

Recall that in Chapter 7, Becoming Super, that we looked at the fundamental difference in the math of millionaires versus the math of the rest of the world: while most of the world works in terms of addition, the wealthy like to *multiply*. In that chapter, we looked at multiplication in the form of leveraging your time through priorities, and through the efforts of others.

But money also needs to multiply. I like to think of money as having a *velocity*. When your money sits in a savings account, its velocity is low—it's taking years to grow. That's *slow money*.

When you invest in a business, or real estate, or find other ways to put your money to work for greater return, your money begins to pick up speed. Its velocity increases, and as a result, so does your wealth.

Money needs to be put to work. If you want to become a millionaire, you'll need to learn to leverage your money.

The higher the velocity of your money, the faster you become a millionaire.

Principle #3: Understand Risk

Generally, however, the higher the velocity of your money, the greater the risk. Think of your money as a car. At low speeds—say, the speed limit that everyone drives at—it's relatively easy to manage and control almost everything. Your risk of an accident is low.

As you increase your speed, however, your risk goes up. When you start taking hairpin turns at twice the legal limit, your risk increases dramatically. You get to your destination faster, but you take more risk along the way.

Money is no different. The faster it goes, the higher your risk. The higher your risk, the faster you can become wealthy, but the greater your chance of a crash along the way.

The money in your savings account is virtually risk-free. But the interest rate is so low that the speed of your money is actually *negative*—it's growing slower than the economy itself. That's the price you pay for having safe and liquid cash.

A successful venture capitalist, on the other hand, has a very high risk of failure on a deal, but when they're successful, they might multiply their money a hundred-fold or more. Higher risk, but higher potential returns, too.

There's no right answer for how much risk to take—risk tolerance is unique to each of us. What you need to know is that there's a relationship between risk and return, and there are no fast *and* risk-free ways to wealth.

Building significant wealth requires an understanding of, and tolerance for, risk.

Principle #4: Multiple Streams of Income

One way to do both things—to increase the velocity of your money while managing your risk—is to have multiple streams of income.

Even successful millionaires with a single business almost always diversify within that business so that it has more than one income stream. The car dealership sells cars, yes, but also provides repair and maintenance services, corporate rental programs and financing. The restaurant might be open for lunch and dinner, but they also do catering and sell frozen take-home versions of their most popular dishes.

Part of the rationale for this is to increase the amount that they can sell to each customer, but it's also a form of risk reduction, and a way to test new markets for profitability. The multiple streams of income increase your wealth, but also decrease your risk by spreading your eggs over multiple baskets.

At age 25, Hal began planning his exit strategy to leave a lucrative hall of fame sales career to pursue his dream of becoming a full-time entrepreneur. While still in his sales position, he started his first business—and his first additional stream of income—when he began offering sales coaching for individual sales reps and sales teams.

Year by year, using the exact step-by-step formula outlined below, Hal has since added nine additional, significant streams of income. These still include private coaching, as well as group coaching programs, writing books, keynote speaking, facilitating paid masterminds, podcasting, foreign publishing, franchising and publishing books in *The Miracle Morning* book series, affiliate income, and hosting live 300+ person events.

Your additional income streams can be active, passive or a combination of the two. Some may pay you for doing work that you love (active), while others can provide income for you without your having to do much of anything at all (passive). You can diversify your income streams among different industries to protect you against major losses during downturns in one market and allow you to financially benefit from the upswings in another.

While Hal's approach to creating multiple streams of income is just one of countless that you could take (i.e., you could buy real estate, leverage the stock market, open brick-and-mortar storefronts, etc.) the following steps give you a practical, straightforward process to start developing your income streams.

What's important is that you make diversifying your sources of income a priority. Schedule time blocks in your schedule—one hour a day, one day a week, or a few hours every Saturday—so that you can begin to establish additional income sources that bring you additional monthly income, which will provide financial security in the present, and ultimately financial freedom in the as-soon-as-possible future.

Here are the steps that Hal has repeatedly implemented, which you can apply or modify to fit your situation:

A. Clarify your unique value.

Every person on this planet has unique gifts, abilities, experiences, and value to offer in a way that adds value for others, and that they can be highly compensated for. Figure out the knowledge, experience, ability or solution you have, or can create, which others will find value in, and gladly pay you for.

Remember, what might be common knowledge to you isn't for other people. Here are a few ways that you can differentiate your value in the marketplace:

Who you are and your unique personality will always differentiate your value from that of every other human being on earth. Many people will resonate with your personality better than they will with someone else offering value that's similar or even the same.

Knowledge is the one thing you can increase relatively quickly. As Tony Robbins wrote in *Money: Master the Game*, "One reason people succeed is that they have knowledge other people don't have. You pay your lawyer or your doctor for the knowledge and skills you lack." Increasing your knowledge in a specific area is an effective way to increase the value that others will pay you for—either to teach them what you know or to apply your knowledge on their behalf.

Packaging is how you can differentiate your value. When Hal wrote *The Miracle Morning*, he admittedly had to overcome his insecurity around the fact that waking up early wasn't exactly something he invented. He wondered if there would even be a market for the book. But as hundreds of thousands of readers have shared, what made the book so impactful is the way that the information was *packaged*. It was simple, and it gave people a step-by-step process that made it possible for anyone to significantly improve any area of their life, by altering how they start their day.

B. Identify your target audience.

Determine who you are best qualified to serve. With his background as a record-breaking sales rep, Hal determined that he was best qualified to serve fellow sales reps, so he launched his first coaching program. Now he serves a much larger, worldwide audience through *The Miracle Morning* book series and Best Year Ever Blueprint live events, and he coaches both first-time and established authors, who want to create seven-figure income streams through their book and backend.

Based on the value you can add for others or the problems you can help people solve, who will pay you for the value you can add for them, the solution you can provide, or the results you can help them generate?

C. Build a self-sustaining community.

A turning point in Hal's financial life came when he heard self-made multimillionaire Dan Kennedy explain why one of the most valuable assets you'll ever have, as an entrepreneur, is your email list. At that time, Hal's email list was non-existent beyond his family and friends. Once he understood the potential, he made it a priority. Ten years later, in addition to taking Dan's advice and growing his email list to well over 100,000 loyal subscribers, he took it a step further by launching and growing one of the most engaged online communities in the world.

The Miracle Morning Community Facebook has become a case study, currently with over 100,000 members from 70+ countries, and growing every day.

D. Create a solution.

After your community members tell you what they need, it's your golden opportunity to get to work and create it. This could be a physical or digital product (a book, an audio , a video, a written training program or software) or a service (dog grooming, babysitting, coaching, consulting, speaking or training).

E. Plan the launch.

Think about how Apple rolls out its products. The company doesn't just throw a product on the shelf or its website. No, the company makes it into an event. Apple builds anticipation months in advance, so much so that people are willing to camp out in front of stores for weeks to be the first in line. Do that. To learn how, read the definitive book on the topic, *Launch* by Jeff Walker.

F. Find a mentor.

Depending on your experience level, you may want to make this your first step. As you're aware, one of the most effective methods of minimizing your learning curve and maximizing the speed at which you attain the desired result is to find someone who has already achieved that result and then model their strategy. Rather than try to figure it all out on your own, find someone who has already achieved what you want, determine how this person did it, model this behavior and modify it to fit your needs.

While you may seek a face-to-face or virtual relationship with a mentor, you could also join a mastermind, and/or hire a coach. Even reading a book, like this one, is tapping into the wisdom of a mentor.

Multiple streams of income increase your wealth
while reducing your risk.

Wealth-Building with Real Estate

While Hal generates much of his wealth through the Miracle Morning brand and its associated products and services, I've built the vast majority of mine through real estate.

There is an infinite number of ways to create value, earn money, and build wealth, but real estate deserves a special mention. It's the primary engine of my business, but the best part about real estate is that it can be the primary engine of almost *anyone's* wealth creation efforts. Here's why.

1. **Proven Track Record**. There have been more millionaires created through real estate than in any other way. It's proven time and time again to be an effective way to build wealth, and, unlike some businesses, it's backed by a real asset with real value.

2. **Low Barrier to Entry.** Don't be fooled by ideas of real estate tycoons and huge condominium towers. One of the most compelling features of real estate is that, contrary to what you might think, you don't need to already be wealthy to get

started. Some businesses require millions to start. With real estate, you can start with what you already have.

3. **Short and Long-Term Returns.** I love the fact that real estate can deliver returns in the short-term in the form of rental income, but in the long run, you can also benefit from the appreciation in real estate value as markets grow and their value increases.

4. **Passive Income.** Running a business can be an all-consuming effort—being an entrepreneur, while rewarding, is an *active* form of generating income. Real estate, however, can be highly passive. I can't tell you how satisfying it can be to have someone *else* pay off a mortgage for you while you do other things!

5. **Any Age, Any Skillset.** Real estate is the great equalizer. It doesn't matter if you're young or old, an entrepreneur or a full-time employee. Still in college? You can rent rooms to your fellow students. Retired? Perfect—you can manage your properties and be even more profitable.

There's a reason why so many people have chosen real estate as their path to wealth—it's accessible, it works, and you don't need any special skills. If you need inspiration, try my book *Wealth Can't Wait*, or Robert Kiyosaki's *Rich Dad's CASHFLOW Quadrant*.

Don't be intimidated by real estate. Start small, and over time, you'll be surprised at the portfolio you can build!

What Money Really Measures

The role of money in becoming a millionaire is a kind of paradox. Money matters, and yet, in a strange way, it doesn't. You need to be at least a little obsessed with money to become a millionaire, but it's not the nature of the game. Money is still just the scoreboard.

But what, exactly, is the scoreboard measuring?

The obvious answer is dollars. Or euros. Or pounds sterling, or pesos or yen or whatever currency your yardstick uses.

But while that can give us a technical definition of wealth, it's not very helpful in the process of *making* the money you need to become a millionaire.

For that, we need to look at money differently. We need to ask different questions. Rather than asking, "How much money do I have?" or "How much can I get?", there's a better set of questions that drive to the heart of *what money is really measuring.*

For me, money has always been a measure of *how much better I'm getting.* And for that, the best questions to ask aren't about how much or how fast or how easy. They're more like these:

- How well have I learned and put to use the lessons of wealth?

- How has my skill as an entrepreneur increased?

- How much value do I bring to the world?

- How can I bring more?

- How can I *become* more?

As my answers to those questions change, so does my income. As I grow, so does my wealth.

So where do you begin? You can ask yourself the same questions. Ask yourself what value you can bring to the world. Ask yourself what you need to learn, do and become in order to build wealth. Instead of asking when the world will show you the money, ask yourself what money has shown *you.*

And, of course, if it isn't abundantly clear by now, there's no better time to ask big questions than first thing in the morning.

Just start. Two years from now, you'll wish you would have started today.

Don't wish, and don't wait.

Start.

❧

Morning Millionaires

Charlie, as a very young lawyer, was probably getting $20 an hour. He thought to himself, "Who's my most valuable client?" And he decided it was himself. So he decided to sell himself an hour each day. He did it early in the morning, working on these construction projects and real estate deals. Everybody should do this, be the client, and then work for other people, too, and sell yourself an hour a day.

—Excerpt from The Snowball: Warren Buffett and the Business of Life, by Alice Schroeder

PART III:

THREE PERSONAL GROWTH PRACTICES TO POWER YOUR PATH TO WEALTH

THE NOT-SO-OBVIOUS MILLIONAIRE PRINCIPLES

— 10 —

Not-So-Obvious Millionaire Principle #1:
SELF-LEADERSHIP

Your level of success will seldom exceed your level of personal development...because success is something you attract by the person you become.

-JIM ROHN

sk a hundred people on the street what you need to be a millionaire, and the most common answer will be *more money*. Ask a classroom full of ten-year-old kids, and you'll probably get a similar answer. And while that answer is true in theory, it's not that helpful. Because most people believe that the only way to get more money is to *work* more.

It's not that work isn't important, but society has conditioned us to think that the *only* way to have more is to do more.

- Want more money? Work harder. Put in *more* hours.
- Want more sex? Lift *more* weight and log *more* steps.
- Want more love? Do *more* for your partner than they do for you.

But what if the real secret to having more of what we want in our lives is not about *doing* more but *becoming* more?

It is this philosophy that gave birth to, and remains the foundation of, the Miracle Morning: that your level of success *in every single area of your life* is always determined by your level of *personal development* —things like your beliefs, knowledge, emotional intelligence, skills, abilities, faith, etc.

In other words, *if you want to have more, you must first become more.*

The fundamental principle of the Miracle Morning is that who you're becoming is far more important than what you're doing. But the irony is that what you're doing each day is also determining who you're becoming. To become more, you need to carefully reflect on how you're spending your time and energy.

Millionaires, whether they realize it or not, *are self-leaders.* They embrace the idea that they must become more, and the key to that development lies within. Before I reveal the essential principles of self-leadership, I want to share with you what I've discovered about the crucial role that *mindset* plays as the foundation of effective self-leadership and, in turn, wealth creation.

Be Aware—and Skeptical—of Your Self-Imposed Limitations

You may be holding on to false limiting beliefs that are unconsciously interfering with your ability to achieve your personal and professional goals.

For example, you may be someone who repeats, "I wish I were more organized." Yet you are more than capable of providing the structure and inspiration to be organized. Thinking of yourself as less-than-capable assumes imminent failure and simultaneously thwarts your ability to succeed. Life contains enough obstacles without you creating more for yourself!

Effective self-leaders closely examine their beliefs, decide which ones serve them, and eliminate those that don't.

When you find yourself stating anything that sounds like a limiting belief, from "I don't have enough time" to "I could never do that," pause and turn your self-limiting statements into empowering questions, such as the following: *Where can I find more time in my schedule? How might I be able to do that?*

Doing this allows you to tap into your inborn creativity and find solutions. You can always find a way when you're committed. As tennis star Martina Navratilova said, "The difference between involvement and commitment is like ham and eggs. The chicken is involved; the pig is committed." Being all in is the key to making anything happen.

See Yourself as Better than You've Ever Been

As Hal wrote in *The Miracle Morning*, most of us suffer from Rearview Mirror Syndrome, limiting our current and future results based on who we were in the past. Remember that, although *where you are is a result of who you were, where you go depends entirely on the person you choose to be, from this moment forward.* This is especially important for millionaires. You will make mistakes. Don't let your sense of guilt about that keep you from seeing that you're capable of more than you've yet to imagine. There are few limits to who you can become and what you can create for your life. Every mistake provides an opportunity for you to learn, grow, and become better than you've ever been before.

I watched an interview with Sara Blakely, the founder of Spanx, who is the youngest self-made female billionaire in the United States. She attributes her success to a mindset her father instilled in her. "When I was growing up, he encouraged us to fail. We'd come home from school, and at dinner, he'd say: 'What did you fail at today?' And if there was nothing, he'd be disappointed. It was an interesting kind of reverse psychology. I would come home and say that I tried out for something and I was just horrible and he high-fived me." If we allow them to be, our mistakes can turn into our greatest lessons.

We all make mistakes. As human beings, we do not come with instruction manuals, and there will always be someone with an unsolicited opinion about the way you are living your life. Don't listen to the static! Be confident in your choices, and when you aren't sure, find the answers and support you need.

All successful people, at some point, made a choice to see themselves as better than they had ever been before. They stopped maintaining limiting beliefs based on their past and instead started forming beliefs based on their unlimited potential.

One of the best ways to do this is to follow the four-step Miracle Morning affirmations formula that was outlined in chapter 3 to create results-oriented affirmations. Be sure to create affirmations that reinforce what's possible for you by reminding you of your ideal outcome, why it's important to you, which actions you're committed to taking to achieve it, and precisely when you're committed to taking those actions.

Actively Seek Support

Seeking support is crucial for millionaires, yet many people struggle, suffering in silence because they assume everyone else has greater capabilities.

People who are self-leaders know they can't do it alone. You might need moral support, for example, so you can replenish the energy stores that life is so famous for depleting. Or you may need accountability support to overcome your tendency to disengage when the going gets tough. We all need support in different areas of our lives, and great self-leaders understand that and use it to their benefit.

The Miracle Morning Community on Facebook is a great place to start looking for support. The members are positive and responsive. Try joining a local group for people with similar goals and interests. Meetup.com can help you find like-minded folks who are close by. I highly recommend getting an accountability partner and, if you can, a life or business coach to help you.

The Four Foundational Principles of Self-Leadership

While self-leadership is a skill, all skills are built on a foundation of principles. To grow and reach your desired levels of success, you'll need to become a proficient self-leader.

My favorite way to cut the learning curve in half and decrease the time it takes for you to reach the top one percent is to model the traits and behaviors of those who have reached the top before you.

During my years of wealth building, I've seen many millionaires and a myriad of effective strategies. Here are the four principles I believe will make the biggest impact on your commitment to self-leadership.

Principle #1: Take 100 Percent Responsibility

Here's the hard truth: if your life and business are not where you want them to be, it's all on you.

The sooner you take ownership of that fact, the sooner you'll begin to move forward. This isn't meant to be harsh. Successful people are rarely victims. In fact, one of the reasons they are successful is that they take absolute, total, and complete responsibility for every single aspect of their lives—whether it's personal or professional, good or bad, their job or someone else's.

While victims habitually waste their time and energy blaming others and complaining, achievers are busy creating the results and circumstances they want for their lives. While mediocre entrepreneurs complain that none of their prospects are buying for *this* reason or *that* reason, or grumble that it's their team's fault for underperforming, successful entrepreneurs take 100 percent responsibility for finding the right prospects and, more importantly, acquiring the skills necessary to build volume and get people started correctly. They're so busy working that they don't have time to complain.

I've heard Hal articulate a profound distinction, during one of his keynote speeches: "The moment you take 100 percent responsibility for everything in your life is the same moment you claim your power to change anything in your life. However, the crucial distinction is to realize that taking responsibility is not the same thing as accepting *blame*. While blame determines who is at fault for something, responsibility determines who is committed to improving a situation. It rarely matters who is at fault. All that matters is that YOU are committed to improving your situation." He's right. And it's so empowering when you start to think and act accordingly. Suddenly, your life and your results are within your control.

When you take ownership of your life, there's no time for discussing whose fault something is, or who gets the blame. Playing the blame game is easy, but there's no longer any place for it in your life. Finding reasons why you didn't meet your goals is for the other guy, not you. You own your results—good and bad. You can celebrate the good and learn from the so-called bad. Either way, you always have a choice about how you respond or react in any and every situation.

One of the reasons this mindset is so important is that you are leading by example. If you're always looking for someone to blame, your team sees that, and they likely don't respect it. Like a parent trying to bring out the best in their kids, the people you lead are always watching you, and it's crucial to live by the values that you want to instill in each of them.

Here's the psychological shift I suggest you make: take ownership and stewardship over all of your decisions, actions, and outcomes, starting right now. Replace unnecessary blame with unwavering responsibility. Even if someone else drops that ball, ask yourself what you could have done—and, more importantly, what you can do in the future—to prevent that ball from being dropped again. While you can't change what's in the past, the good news is that you can change everything else.

From now on, there's no doubt about who is at the wheel, and who is responsible for all of your results. You make the calls, do the follow-up, decide the outcomes you want, and then get them. Your results are 100 percent your responsibility.

Remember: you are in the position of power, you are in control, and there are no limits to what you can accomplish.

Principle #2: Prioritize Fitness and Make Exercise Enjoyable

On a scale of one to ten, where would you rank your health and fitness? Are you fit? Strong? Do you *feel* good, more often than not?

How about your energy level throughout the day? Do you have more energy than you know what to do with? Can you wake up before your alarm and do what's important, handle all the demands of the day, and put out the inevitable fires, all without struggling to make it through the day without feeling exhausted and out of breath?

We covered exercise as the *E* in S.A.V.E.R.S., and yes, I'm going to discuss it again right now. It's a fact that the state of your health and fitness is a huge factor in your energy and success levels—especially for entrepreneurs. Because, unlike employees, you're not paid based on the times you clock in and out. You're paid based on the quality of the results you produce within the time that you work. Being a millionaire is an energy sport. Like any sport, you need an extraordinary supply of stamina in order to excel.

It's no surprise, then, that three priorities of top performers, each of which you must prioritize in your life, are the quality of their food, their sleep, and their exercise. We'll delve deeper into each in the next chapter on energy engineering, but let's start with making sure you get your daily exercise in. The key is to find physical activities that you enjoy doing.

The correlation between physical fitness, happiness, and success are undeniable. It is no coincidence that you rarely see top performers who are terribly out of shape. Most schedule and invest thirty to sixty minutes of their time each day to hit the gym or the running trail, because they understand the important role that daily exercise plays in their success.

While the *E* in S.A.V.E.R.S. ensures that you're going to start each day with five to ten minutes of exercise, we recommended that you commit to engaging in additional thirty- to sixty-minute workouts, at least three to five times per week. Doing so will ensure that your fitness level supports the energy and confidence you need to succeed.

Even better is to engage in some form of exercise that brings you a deep level of enjoyment. That might mean going for a hike in nature, playing ultimate Frisbee, or getting an exercise bike and putting it in front of your TV so you can enjoy your favorite TV episode and forget that you're even exercising. Or, do what Hal does;

he loves wakeboarding and playing basketball—two excellent forms of exercise—so he does one of them, every single workday. You'll see Hal's foundational schedule in the coming pages, so you know how those activities fit with the rest of his priorities.

Which physical activities do you enjoy, that you can commit to schedule as part of your daily exercise ritual?

Principle #3: Systematize Your World

Effective self-leaders have *systems* for just about everything, from work activities—such as scheduling, following up, entering orders, and sending thank-you cards—to personal activities, such as sleeping, eating, managing money, maintaining cars, and taking care of family responsibilities. Those systems make life easier and ensure you are ready for anything.

Here are a few practices you can implement immediately to begin systematizing your world:

1. Automation—In my household, milk, eggs, and bread are necessities, but constantly needing to stop at the grocery store for replenishments became burdensome. I discovered a service that delivers groceries, so we decided to have them delivered to us instead of running out all the time for more. If you find something in your life that does not bring you joy, try to eliminate it through automation.

I hate cleaning toilets and doing the laundry. So, I found a way to hire help for those chores. One benefit of that is that it makes us accountable for keeping the house clutter-free. I realize housekeepers may not be in the budget for everyone, but if you can't yet afford one, you may be able to trade services with friends or come up with other creative solutions. One of my friends includes house cleaning as the exercise portion of the Life S.A.V.E.R.S., so a little gets done every morning.

2. Briefcases and Beyond—Hal, in addition to being a best-selling author, is a speaker who travels week after week, sharing *The Miracle Morning* message with audiences around the country and abroad. Collecting the items he needed for every trip was time-consuming, inefficient, and ineffective because he would often forget something at home or in his office. After the third time he forgot the charger for his computer and had to find an Apple store to buy a $99 replacement (ouch) or ask the front desk for a phone charger, shaver, or an extra set of cufflinks left behind by a previous guest, he'd had enough. He assembled a travel bag containing every item he needs for his trips, and now he can leave at a moment's notice because his bag contains everything to conduct business on the road: business cards, brochures, copies of his books, adapters, and chargers for his phone and computer. He even includes earplugs in case his hotel room neighbor is noisy.

You'll know you need a system when you have a recurring challenge or find that you're missing important items because you're unprepared. If you're walking out the door with just enough time to get to your first destination of the day on schedule only to discover your car is running on fumes, you need a system for getting out the door earlier. Here are some ways to plan ahead:

Pack your lunch, your purse or briefcase, and your gym bag the night before, and lay out your outfit for the next day.

Prepare an out-of-office kit with brochures, catalogs, or other items you need for business.

Stash healthy snacks for when you're on the go (apples, kale chips, carrots, etc.) to prevent stopping at a convenience store or fast-food joint for a not-so-healthy option.

Said another way, wherever you need to get your act together, you need a system. A life without systems is a life of unnecessary stress! This is especially true for millionaires.

3. Foundational Scheduling—The use of a foundational schedule is key to maximizing your focus, productivity, and income. If we spend too many days bouncing around from one task to another and end far too many days wondering where in the hell the time went and what, if any, significant progress was made, we've missed more key opportunities than we can calculate. Can you relate?

I am going to share with you—or at least remind you of—something that will transform your ability to produce consistent and spectacular results. *You must create a foundational schedule that gives structure and intentionality to your days and weeks.* A foundational schedule is a pre-determined, recurring schedule that is made up of focused time-blocks, which are each dedicated to your highest-priority activities. Most of us intuitively understand the benefits of this, but very few do it effectively on a consistent basis.

I know, I know—you became an adult to get away from structure. Trust me; I get it. But the more you leverage a foundational schedule, consisting of time-blocks—typically ranging from one to three hours each—that are dedicated to focusing on the projects or activities that will help you make the most of your life and business—the more freedom you'll ultimately create.

That's not to say you cannot have flexibility in your schedule. In fact, I strongly suggest that you *schedule* flexibility. Plan plenty of time-blocks for family, fun, and recreation into your calendar. You could even go as far as to include a "whatever I feel like" time-block, during which you do, well … whatever you feel like. You can also move things on occasion as needed. What's important is that you go through your days and weeks with a high level of clarity and intentionality with regard to how you're going to invest every hour of every day, even if that hour is spent doing *whatever you feel like.* At least you planned on it. Maintaining a foundational schedule is how you will ensure that you maximize your productivity so that you almost never end the day wondering where in the hell your time went. It won't go anywhere without you making a conscious decision because you'll be intentional with every minute of it.

I asked Hal to share his weekly foundational schedule so you can see an example of what this can look like. Although Hal has the luxury of entrepreneurial freedom and doesn't need to follow any pre-determined schedule, he will tell you that having this foundational schedule in place is one of his keys to ensuring he maximizes each day.

HAL'S FOUNDATIONAL SCHEDULE

Time	Mon	Tues
4:00 AM	SAVERS	SAVERS
5:00 AM	Write	Write
6:00 AM	Emails	Emails
7:00 AM	Take kids to school	Take kids to school
8:00 AM	Staff Mtg.	#1 Priority
9:00 AM	#1 Priority	Wakeboard
↓	↓	↓
11:00 AM	Lunch	Lunch
12:00 PM	Basketball	Priorities
1:00 PM	Priorities	Interview
2:00 PM	Priorities	Interview
3:00 PM	Priorities	Interview
4:00 PM	Priorities	Priorities
5:00 PM	FAMILY	FAMILY
↓	↓	↓
10:00 PM	Bed	Bed

(Note: Every hour is planned.)

Wed	Thurs	Fri	Sat/Sun
SAVERS	SAVERS	SAVERS	SAVERS
Write	Write	Write	Write
Emails	Emails	Emails	↓
Take kids to school	Take kids to school	Take kids to school	FAMILY Time
#1 Priority	#1 Priority	#1 Priority	↓
↓	Wakeboard	↓	↓
↓	↓	↓	↓
Lunch	Lunch	Lunch	↓
Basketball	Priorities	Basketball	↓
Client Call	Interview	Priorities	↓
Client Call	Interview	Priorities	↓
Client Call	Interview	Priorities	↓
Priorities	Priorities	PLANNING	↓
FAMILY	FAMILY	Date Night	↓
↓	↓	↓	↓
Bed	Bed	:^) ???	Bed

Keep in mind that, as happens to most everyone, things come up that cause Hal's foundational schedule to change (events, speaking engagements, vacations, etc.), but only temporarily. As soon as he's back home and in his office, this is the schedule that he falls back into.

One of the main reasons that this technique is so effective is because it takes the emotional roller coaster, caused by varied results, out of the decision-making for your daily activities. How many times has an appointment gone bad and then affected your emotional state and your ability to focus? Chances are, your focus and productivity were hindered for the rest of that day. If you had followed your foundational schedule, though, and the calendar said networking event, writing ads, or making calls, and you were committed to the calendar, then you would have had a fruitful afternoon. Take control. Stop leaving your productivity up to chance and letting outside influences manage your calendar. Create your foundational schedule—one that incorporates everything you need to get done, as well as recreational, family and fun time—and follow through with it, no matter what.

If you find you need additional support to ensure that you follow through, send a copy of your foundational schedule to an accountability partner or your coach, and have them hold you accountable. Your commitment to this one system will allow you to have significantly more control over your productivity and results.

Principle #4: Commit to Consistency

If there is any not-so-obvious secret to success, this is it: *commit to consistency*. Every result that you desire—from improving your physique to increasing the size of your business to spending more quality time with your family—requires a consistent approach to produce the desired results.

In the chapters that follow, I'll give you the insight and direction you need to take consistent action. For now, prepare your mind to keep going—even when the results you want aren't coming fast enough—and to have the stamina to withstand plenty of rejection and disappointment as you adjust to your new self. The best wealth creators are consistent, persistent, and unfailing in their dedication to taking action every day, and you need to be the same!

How is Your Self-Esteem Doing?

As American playwright August Wilson suggested, "Confront the dark parts of yourself and work to banish them with illumination and forgiveness. Your willingness to wrestle with your demons will cause your angels to sing." Self-esteem gives you the courage to try new things and the power to believe in yourself.

It is vitally important that you permit yourself to feel proud of yourself. Yes, we need to be realistic about our weaknesses and always strive to improve, but don't hesitate to be proud of your strengths and revel in the little wins. In the meantime, many days are filled with disappointments, delays, and denials, so it is vitally important that you love yourself. If you are doing the best you can, give yourself credit. I keep a special section in my journal to write love notes to myself. On days I need a little extra encouragement, I write down all the things I love and appreciate about me.

An unstoppable self-esteem is a powerful tool. You probably already know that with a negative attitude you are going nowhere— and fast! With the right attitude, all the challenges of the day can roll off your back. You stay calm and can keep going. When you are confident in your abilities and committed to consistency, your behavior will change, and your success is inevitable.

Putting Self-Leadership into Action

Developing self-leadership helps put you in the leadership role of your life. It eliminates the victim mentality and ensures you know the values, beliefs, and vision you want to live in.

Step One: Review and integrate the Four Foundational Principles of Self-Leadership:

1. **Take 100 Percent Responsibility.** Remember, the moment you accept responsibility for *everything* in your life is the moment you claim the power to change *anything* in your life. Your success is 100 percent up to you.

2. **Prioritize Fitness and Make Exercise Enjoyable.** If daily fitness isn't already a priority in your life, make it so. In addition to your morning exercise, block time for longer, thirty- to sixty-minute workouts three to five times each week. As for which foods will give you a surplus of energy, we'll cover that in the next chapter.

3. **Systematize Your World.** Start by creating a foundational schedule, and then identify which area of your life or business can benefit by you putting systems and time-blocked schedules in place so that every day your result-producing processes have been predetermined and your success is virtually guaranteed. Most importantly, make sure you instill some system for accountability into your world, whether that be through a colleague or a coach, or by leveraging your team by making commitments to them and leading by example.

4. **Commit to Consistency.** Everyone needs structure. Choose consistency and commit to personal expectations and values. If you're trying a new approach, give it an extended period to work before throwing in the towel to try something different.

Step Two: Develop your self-control and upgrade your self-image by using affirmations and visualization. Be sure to customize both at your earliest opportunity—it takes time to see results, and the sooner you start, the sooner you'll notice improvements.

By now, I hope you've gained a sense of how important your personal development is in creating success. As you continue to read this book—and I suggest you read it more than once—I recommend that you intentionally address the areas where you know you need improvement and expansion. If your self-esteem could use a boost, then take steps to elevate it. Design affirmations to increase and develop it over time. Visualize yourself acting with more confidence, raising your standards, and loving yourself more.

If this sounds overwhelming, remember the power of incremental change. You don't have to do everything all at once. And I've got more good news for you. In the next chapter, we're going to break down exactly how to engineer your life to create optimum levels of sustained physical, mental, and emotional energy so that you're able to maintain extraordinary levels of clarity, focus, and action, day in and day out.

᏶

Morning Millionaires

I get up around 8:00 a.m. and I have one other simple rule: Do one thing in the morning before checking email. It could be showering; it could be going for a long run, it could be jotting some thoughts down in my journal, it's usually writing. Most mornings I try to write for one to two hours before I start the rest of the day (and the to-do list I made the day before).

—Ryan Holiday, bestselling author and media strategist

11

NOT-SO-OBVIOUS MILLIONAIRE PRINCIPLE #2:
ENERGY ENGINEERING

The world belongs to the energetic.
-RALPH WALDO EMERSON

Becoming a millionaire often means that you live and die by your own steam. No matter how you decide to earn, invest, and grow, creating value means approaching your day with a surplus of physical, mental, and emotional vitality.

The trouble is that steam can run low. On some days—and I know you've had these days—you wake up and don't have the drive or motivation you need to meet the challenges you know are coming. Running a startup, growing a company, building a business—it can be exhausting, both physically and mentally, and that's on the good days. To maintain your focus amid uncertainty and overwhelm is no easy task. The good days take enthusiasm, planning, and persistence. The hard days take all that and more.

Becoming wealthy requires an abundance of energy. There's no way around it. You can have the best business plan, the best team, and the best product, but if you don't have the drive to take advantage of those things, reaching your goals is going to be unnecessarily difficult. If you want to maximize your wealth, you need energy—the more the better, and the more *consistent* the better.

- Energy is the fuel that enables you to maintain clarity, focus, and action, so that you can generate stellar results, day after day.

- Energy is contagious—it spreads from you to the world around you like a positive virus, creating symptoms of enthusiasm and positive responses everywhere.

- Energy is the foundation of everything, and it is what determines the success we attract.

The question, then, is *how do you strategically engineer your life so that you maintain high levels of physical, mental and emotional energy*—a sustainable surplus which is always available to you on demand?

A common approach when we struggle with this issue is trying to compensate with caffeine, sugar and other stimulants. They'll often work for a while until we crash. You may have noticed that you can lean on stimulants to sustain you for a short while, but then the effect wears off just when you need it the most.

I can just hear one of those infomercial hosts chime in here: *but David, there's got to be a better way!*

In fact, there is. If you've been fueling yourself on coffee and pure determination, you've been missing out on what's possible when you understand how energy works and commit to engineering your life to optimize it.

Natural Energy Cycles

The first thing to understand is that the goal here isn't to be running at full speed all the time. It isn't practical to maintain a constant output. As human beings, we have a natural ebb and flow to our drive. Be aware of when you experience your energetic peaks through the day, and give yourself the time to rest, rejuvenate, and recharge when the intensity lessens.

Just like houseplants need water, human beings need regular replenishing. You can go full tilt for long periods of time, but eventually, your mind, body, and spirit will need to be refilled. Think of your life as a container that holds your energy. When you don't properly manage your container, it's like having a hole in the bottom. No matter how much you pour in, you'll never catch up.

Instead of letting yourself get to the point of being overwhelmed, burned out, or stressed out, why not become proactive and have an auto-recharge system in place? This will help you plug the holes in your container and allow you to fill up with the energy you need.

Being continually exhausted is unacceptable; you don't have to settle for it. You don't have to resign yourself to being tired, cranky, behind on your to-do list, out of shape, and unhappy. There are a few simple ways to strategically engineer your life for optimal and sustainable physical, mental, and emotional vitality.

Here are the three principles I follow to keep my energy levels at maximum capacity and on tap for whenever I need them.

1. Eat and Drink for Energy

When it comes to generating a surplus of sustainable energy, what you eat and drink may play the most critical role of all. If you're like most people, you base your food choices on taste first, and consequences second (if you consider them at all). Yet, what pleases our taste buds at the moment often doesn't give us the energy we need to last throughout the day.

There is nothing wrong with eating foods that taste good, but if you want to be healthy and perform like a champion, it's crucial that you make a conscious decision to *place more value on the consequences of the foods you eat than you do on the taste*. Why? Because your food choices are among the most energy-impacting decisions that you make. Take a second to think about how exhausted you feel after a big meal (see: Thanksgiving dinner). It's no coincidence that a large meal is usually followed by heavy eyes and ultimately a nap. It's called a "food coma" for a reason.

Highly processed foods—packaged goods made from high amounts of sugar and other simple carbohydrates—drain us more than they fuel us. Rather than increasing your energy, these essentially "dead" foods cause you to spike and then crash, leaving you tired and listless. On the other hand, whole foods like fruits, vegetables, nuts, and seeds typically keep you healthier and maintain your energy levels, empowering your body and mind and enabling you to perform at your best.

Everything you put into your body either contributes to or detracts from your health and stamina. Drinking water puts a check in the plus column. Double shots of tequila won't. Eating a diet rich in fresh fruits and vegetables equals more plusses. Rolling through the drive-through to wolf down some fast food? Not so much. This isn't rocket science, but it may be the single most important area of your life to optimize, and if you're like most people, you may need to stop fooling yourself.

If you're not already doing so, it's time to be intentional and strategic about what you eat, when you eat, and, most importantly— *why* you eat—so that you can engineer your life for optimal vibrancy.

Strategic Eating

Up until this point, you may have been wondering, *when the heck do I get to eat during my Miracle Morning?* I'll cover that here. We'll also address *what* to eat for peak performance, which is critical, and *why* you choose to eat what you eat—which may be most important consideration of all.

When to Eat – Digesting food is a process that requires energy. The bigger the meal and the more food you give your body to digest, the more drained you may feel. I recommend eating your first meal *after* your Miracle Morning. This ensures that, for optimum alertness and focus during the S.A.V.E.R.S., your blood will be flowing to your brain rather than to your stomach to digest your food.

Some people are hungrier than others in the morning. You may want to start your day by ingesting a small amount of healthy fat as fuel for your brain. Studies show that keeping your mind sharp and your moods in balance may be largely related to the type of fat you eat. "Our brain is at least 60 percent fat, and it's composed of fats (like omega-3s) that must be obtained from the diet," says Amy Jamieson-Petonic, MEd, a registered dietitian, the director of wellness coaching at the Cleveland Clinic and a national spokesperson for the American Dietetic Association.

After drinking his first full glass of water, Hal starts every morning with healthy fats, which typically include either eating a tablespoon of organic coconut oil (specifically *Nutiva Organic Coconut Manna*, which you can order from Amazon.com), or he blends a cup of organic coffee with MCT oil (also available on Amazon.com). Both the tablespoon of coconut oil, and the small amount of MCT oil, contain healthy fats to provide fuel for the brain.

The health benefits of cacao are significant, from being a powerhouse full of antioxidants (cacao rates in the top 20 on the oxygen radical absorbance capacity [a.k.a. ORAC] scale, which is used to rate the antioxidant capacity of foods), to lowering blood pressure. Maybe most exciting is that eating cacao makes you happy! It contains *phenylethylamine* (known as the "love drug"), which is responsible for our state of mood and pleasure and delivers the same feelings you get when you are in love. It also acts as a stimulant and can improve mental alertness. In other words, cacao is a big winner in the nutrition department.

If you do feel like you must eat a meal first thing in the morning, make sure that it's a small, light, easily digestible meal, such as fresh fruit or a smoothie (more on that in a minute).

Why to Eat – Let's take a moment to delve deeper into *why* you choose to eat the foods that you do. When you're shopping at the grocery store or selecting food from a menu at a restaurant, what criteria do you use to determine which foods you are going to put into your body? Are your choices based purely on taste? Texture? Convenience? Are they based on health? Stamina? Dietary restrictions?

Most people eat the foods they do based mainly on *taste* and, at a deeper level, based on the emotional attachment to the foods they like the taste of. If you were to ask someone, "Why did you eat that ice cream? Why did you drink that soda?" Or, "Why did you bring that fried chicken home from the grocery store?" You would most likely hear responses like *Mmm because I love ice cream! ... I love the taste of soda! ... I was in the mood for fried chicken!* All of these answers are based on the emotional enjoyment derived primarily from the way these foods taste. In this case, the person is not likely to explain their food choices by describing how much value these foods will add to their health, or how much sustained drive they'll receive as a result of ingesting them.

If you want to perform at your best and maximize your productivity each day (we all do), and if you want your life to be healthy and disease-free (who doesn't?), then it is crucial that you reexamine why you eat the foods that you do. It bears repeating: from this point forward, *start placing significantly more value on the consequences of the foods you eat than you place on the taste.* The taste only provides you with a few minutes of pleasure, but the health and stamina consequences impact the rest of your day and, ultimately, the rest of your life.

This doesn't mean you have to eat foods that *don't* taste good in exchange for health and energy benefits; the beauty of food is that you can have both taste *and* energy. But if you want to live every day with an abundance of energy so you can perform at your best and live a long, healthy life, you must choose foods with health and sustained energy as your top priority.

What to Eat – Before we talk about what to eat, let's take a second to talk about what to *drink*. Remember that step four of the Five-Step Snooze-Proof Wake-Up Strategy is to drink a glass of water first thing in the morning so you can rehydrate and reenergize after a full night of sleep.

As for what to eat, it has been proven that a diet rich in *living foods*, such as fresh fruits and vegetables, will greatly increase your vitality, improve your mental focus and emotional well-being, keep you healthy, and protect you from disease. So, Hal created a Miracle Morning *super-food smoothie* that incorporates everything your body needs in one tall, frosty glass! Hal's smoothie contains complete proteins (*all* of the essential amino acids), age-defying antioxidants, omega-3 essential fatty acids (to boost immunity, cardiovascular health, and brain power), plus a rich spectrum of vitamins and minerals, and that's just for starters. There are also *super-foods*, such as the stimulating, mood-lifting phytonutrients in cacao (the tropical bean from which chocolate is made), the long-lasting energy-support of maca (the Andean adaptogen revered for its hormone-balancing effects), and the immune-boosting nutrients and appetite-suppressing properties of chia seeds.

The Miracle Morning Super-Food Smoothie not only provides you with sustained energy, but it also tastes great. You might even find that it enhances your ability to create miracles in your everyday life. You can download and print the recipe for free at www.TMMBook. com, along with the other resources. That way you can keep the printed recipe (and not this book) by your blender. Because, if you're like me, you'll occasionally forget to secure the lid and end up with super-food smoothie all over your kitchen.

Remember the old saying *you are what you eat?* It's true. Take care of your body so your body will take care of you.

I have shifted my view of food from that of a reward, treat, or comfort, to that of fuel. I want to eat delicious, healthy foods that support my mission and allow me to keep going as long as I need to go. And I still enjoy certain foods that are not the healthiest choices, but I strategically reserve them for times when I don't need to maintain optimum power levels, such as evenings and weekends.

The easiest way for me to start making better decisions about my eating was to begin paying attention to the way I felt after eating certain foods. I started setting a timer for sixty minutes after I finished each meal. One hour later, my timer went off, and I assessed how I felt. It didn't take long for me to recognize which foods gave me the biggest power boost and which ones didn't. I can clearly tell the difference in my energy level on the days when I drink a smoothie or eat a salad, and the days I cave and eat a chicken sandwich or some of that pizza that smells so good. The former options give me a surplus of energy, while the latter put me in an energy deficit.

What would it be like to give your body what it needs to work and play for as long as you like? What would it be like to give yourself exactly what you deserve? Give yourself the gift of great health, consciously chosen through what you eat and drink.

If you are eating throughout the day almost as an afterthought, maybe hitting a drive-through after you've reached the point of being famished, it is time to start building a new strategy.

Give some thought to the following questions:

- Can I start to consciously consider the consequences (both in health and stamina) of what I eat, and can I value that above the taste?

- Can I keep water with me so that I can hydrate with intention and purpose and avoid becoming dehydrated?

- Can I plan my meals in, including incorporating healthy snacks, so I can combat any patterns I have that don't serve me?

Yes, you can do all of these, and much more. Think about how much better your life will be and how much more energy you will have for your business when you become conscious and intentional about your eating and drinking habits.

- You will maintain a positive mental and emotional state. Low energy causes us to feel down, whereas high energy levels produce a positive state of mind, outlook, and attitude.

- You will be more disciplined. Low energy drains our willpower, making us more likely to choose to do the *easy* things over the *right* things. High energy levels increase our level of self-discipline.

- You will live longer.

- You will set an example for the people you lead, and the people you love. How we live our lives gives permission to those around us to do the same.

- You will get healthier, feel much better, and live longer.

- Bonus—You will settle at your natural weight effortlessly.

- Best Bonus Ever—You'll grow your business faster, make more sales, recruit more and better team members, and make more money because you'll look and feel great!

Don't forget to stay hydrated throughout the day. Lack of water can lead to dehydration, a condition that occurs when you don't have enough water in your body to carry out normal functions. Even mild dehydration can drain your vitality and make you feel tired.

By implementing the Five-Step Snooze-Proof Wake-Up Strategy, you'll have had your first glass of water at the start of the day. Beyond that, I recommend keeping a large water bottle with you and making a habit of drinking sixteen ounces every one to two hours. If remembering is a challenge for you, set a recurring timer or add multiple alarms on your phone to hold you accountable. Every time you hear a reminder, drink what's left in your water bottle and refill it for the next round of rehydration. Keeping a full bottle with you will allow you to take in water as needed as well.

When it comes to frequency of eating, it's important to refuel every three to four hours, with small, easily digestible, living foods. My regular meals consist of some form of protein and vegetables. To keep my blood glucose levels from dropping, I frequently snack on living foods, including raw fruits and nuts, and one of my favorite go-to snacks—kale chips. I try to plan my best meals for the days I need to be the most productive.

I believe that eating for energy—from my first meal of the day until I'm done working—combined with exercise also gives me the freedom to eat what I want, in the evenings and on weekends. I believe I can eat whatever I want, just not always as much as I'd like. I've learned to taste everything, but to eat just enough that I'm satisfied.

In the end, here is the simple thing to remember: food is fuel. We must commit to using the best fuel possible to get us from the beginning of the day all the way to the end, feeling great and having plenty of energy. Placing more value on the consequences of the foods you eat above the taste, along with eating healthy fats and living foods that give you high-octane fuel, is the first step in energy engineering.

2. Sleep and Wake to Win

Sleep more to achieve more. That might be the most counterintuitive business mantra you'll ever hear, but it's true. The body needs enough shut-eye each night to function properly and to recharge after a demanding day. Sleep also plays a critical role in immune function, metabolism, memory, learning, and other vital body functions. It's when the body does most of its repairing, healing, resting, and growing. If you don't sleep enough, you're gradually wearing yourself down.

Sleeping Versus Sleeping *Enough*

But how much is enough? There is a big difference between the amount of sleep you can get by on and the amount you need to function optimally. Researchers at the University of California, San Francisco discovered that some people have a gene that enables them to do well on six hours of sleep a night. This gene, however, is very rare, appearing in less than 3 percent of the population. For the other 97 percent of us, six hours doesn't come close to cutting it. Just because you're able to function on five to six hours of sleep doesn't mean you wouldn't feel a lot better and get more done if you spent an extra hour or two in bed.

That may sound counterintuitive. I can almost hear you thinking, *spend more time in bed and get more done? How does that work?* But it has been well documented that enough sleep allows the body to function at higher levels of performance. You'll not only work better and faster, but your attitude will improve, too.

The amount of nightly rest each individual needs differs, but research shows that the average adult needs approximately seven to eight hours of sleep to restore the energy it takes to handle all of the demands of living each day.

I have been conditioned, as many of us have, to think I need eight to ten hours of sleep. In fact, sometimes I need less, and sometimes I need more. The best way to figure out if you're meeting your sleep needs is to evaluate how you feel as you go about your day. If you're logging enough hours, you'll feel energetic and alert all day long, from the moment you wake up until your regular bedtime. If you're not, you'll reach for caffeine or sugar mid-morning or mid-afternoon… or both.

If you're like most people, when you don't get enough rest, you have difficulty concentrating, thinking clearly, and remembering things. You might notice your ineffectiveness at home or work and even blame these missteps on your busy schedule. The more sleep you miss, the more pronounced your symptoms become.

In addition, a lack of rest and relaxation can work a number on your mood. Entrepreneurship is no place for crankiness! It is a scientific fact that when individuals miss out on good nightly rest, their personalities are affected, and they are generally grumpier, less patient, and more apt to snap at people. The result of missing out on critical rest might make you a bear to be around, which is not much fun for anyone, yourself included.

Most adults cut back on their sleep to pack more activities into their day. As you run against the clock to beat deadlines, you might be tempted to skimp on sleep in order to get more done. Unfortunately, lack of sleep can cause the body to run down, which allows illnesses, viruses, and diseases the tiny opening they need to attack the body. When you are sleep-deprived, your immune system can become compromised and susceptible to just about anything. Eventually, lack of rest can cause illness that leads to missed days or even weeks of work. That's no way to attempt to grow your business.

On the flip side, when you get enough sleep, your body runs as it should, you're pleasant to be around, and your immune system is stronger. And that's precisely when you'll make more sales and attract more people into your business. Think of good sleep as the time when you turn on your inner magnet. Wake up rested and in a great mood because of your S.A.V.E.R.S., and you'll attract more business because a happy entrepreneur is also a rich one.

The True Benefits of Sleep

You may not realize how powerful sleep is. While you're happily wandering through your dreams, sleep is doing some hard work on your behalf and delivering a host of amazing benefits.

Sleep improves your memory. Your mind is surprisingly busy while you snooze. Sleep allows you to clean out damaging toxins that are byproducts of brain function during the day, strengthen memories and practice skills learned while you were awake through a process called consolidation.

"If you are trying to learn something, whether it's physical or mental, you learn it to a certain point with practice," says sleep expert Dr. David Rapoport, "but something happens while you sleep that makes you learn it better."

In other words, if you're trying to learn something new, whether it's Spanish, a new tennis swing, or the specifications of a new product in your arsenal, you'll perform better when you get adequate sleep.

Sleep can help you live longer. Too much or too little sleep is associated with a shorter lifespan, although it's not clear if it's a cause or an effect. In a 2010 study of women ages fifty to seventy-nine, more deaths occurred in women who got fewer than five hours or more than six-and-a-half hours of sleep per night. Getting the right amount of sleep is a good idea for your long-term health.

Sleep boosts creativity. Get a good night's sleep before grabbing the easel and paintbrushes or the pen and paper. In addition to consolidating memories or making them stronger, your brain appears to reorganize and restructure them, which may result in more creativity as well.

Researchers at Harvard University and Boston College found that people seem to strengthen the emotional components of a memory during sleep, which may help spur the creative process.

Sleep assists in attaining and maintaining a healthy weight more easily. If you're overweight, you won't have the same energy levels as those at a healthy weight. If you are changing your lifestyle to include more exercise and diet modifications, you'll want to plan an earlier bedtime. Putting additional physical demands on your body means you will need to counterbalance those demands with enough rest.

The good news: researchers at the University of Chicago found that dieters who were well rested lost more fat—up to 56 percent more—than those who were sleep-deprived, who lost more muscle mass. Dieters in the study also felt hungrier when they got less sleep. Sleep and metabolism are controlled by the same sectors of the brain, and when you are sleepy, certain hormones—those that drive appetite—go up in your blood.

Sleep lets you feel less stressed. When it comes to our health, stress and sleep are closely connected, and both can affect cardiovascular health. Sleep can reduce stress levels, and with that comes better control of blood pressure. It is also believed that sleep affects cholesterol levels, which play a significant role in heart disease.

Sleep helps prevent mistakes and accidents. The National Highway Traffic Safety Administration reported in 2009 that being tired accounted for the highest number of fatal, single-car, run-off-the-road crashes due to the driver's performance—even more than alcohol! Sleepiness is grossly underrated as a problem by most people, but the cost to our society is enormous. Lack of sleep affects reaction time and decision-making.

If insufficient sleep for only one night can be as detrimental to your driving ability as having an alcoholic drink, imagine how it affects your ability to maintain the focus necessary to become a top entrepreneur.

Getting consistent and effective rest is as critical to performing at your best as what you do or don't have in your diet. A good night's sleep provides the basis for a day of clear thought, sustained energy, and peak performance. You probably already know how many hours you need to be at your best, and it's important that you are optimizing your sleep. However, what may be even more important than how many hours of sleep you get each night is how you approach the act of waking up in the morning.

You Snooze, You Lose: The Truth About Waking Up

The old saying, "you snooze, you lose" may have a much deeper meaning than any of us realized. When you hit the snooze button and delay waking up until you *have* to—meaning you wait to until the time when you have to be somewhere, do something, or take care of someone else—consider that you're starting your day with resistance.

Every time you hit the snooze button, you're in a state of resistance to your day, to your life, and to waking up and creating the life you say you want.

According to Robert S. Rosenberg, medical director of the Sleep Disorders Centers of Prescott Valley and Flagstaff, Arizona, "When you hit the snooze button repeatedly, you're doing two negative things to yourself. First, you're fragmenting what little extra sleep you're getting, so it is of poor quality. Second, you're starting to put yourself through a new sleep cycle that you aren't giving yourself enough time to finish. This can result in persistent grogginess throughout the day."

On the other hand, when you wake up each day with passion and purpose, you join the small percentage of high achievers who are living their dreams. Most importantly, you will be happy. By changing your approach to waking up in the morning, you will change everything. But don't take my word for it—trust these famous early risers: Oprah Winfrey, Tony Robbins, Bill Gates, Howard Schultz, Deepak Chopra, Wayne Dyer, Thomas Jefferson, Benjamin Franklin, Albert Einstein, Aristotle, and far too many more to list here.

No one ever taught us that by learning how to consciously set our intention to wake up each morning with a genuine desire—even enthusiasm—to do so, we could change our entire lives.

If you're just snoozing every day until the last possible moment you have to head off to work, show up for school, or take care of your family, and then coming home and zoning out in front of the television until you go to bed (this used to be my daily routine), I've got to ask you: *When are you going to develop yourself into the person you need to be to create the levels of health, wealth, happiness, success, and freedom that you want and deserve? When are you going to live your life instead of numbly going through the motions looking for every possible distraction to escape reality? What if your reality—your life—could finally be something that you can't wait to be conscious for?*

If you're not already, make sure you start following the Five-Minute Snooze Proof Wake-Up Strategy in chapter 2, and you'll be poised to win. If getting to bed on time is your challenge, try setting a *bedtime alarm* that sounds an hour before your ideal bedtime, prompting you to start winding down so you can hit the sack.

There is no better day than today for us to give up who we've been for who we can become and upgrade the life we've been living for the one we want. There is no better book than the one you are holding in your hands to show you how to become the person you need to be who is capable of quickly attracting, creating and sustaining the life you have always wanted.

How Much Sleep Do We *Really* Need?

The first thing experts will tell you about how many hours of sleep we need is that there is no universal number. The ideal duration of sleep varies from person to person and is influenced by factors such as age, genetics, stress, overall health, how much exercise a person gets, our diet—including how late we eat our last meal—and countless other factors.

For example, if your diet consists of fast food, processed foods, excessive sugar, etc., then your body will be challenged to recharge while you sleep, as it will be working all night to detoxify and filter out the poisons that you've put into it. On the other hand, if you eat a clean diet made up of living food, as we covered in the last section, then your body will recharge and rejuvenate much more easily. The person who eats a clean diet will almost always wake feeling refreshed and with more energy—and able to function optimally, even with less sleep—than the person who eats poorly.

You should also keep in mind that there is such a thing as too much sleep. According to the National Sleep Foundation, some research has found that long sleep durations (nine hours or more) are associated with increased morbidity (illness, accidents) and even mortality (death). This research also found that variables such as depression were significantly associated with long sleep.

Since there is such a wide variety of opposing evidence from countless studies and experts, and since the amount of sleep needed varies from person to person, I'm not going to attempt to make a case that there is one right approach to sleep. Instead, I'll share my real-world results, from personal experience and experimentation, and from studying the sleep habits of some of the greatest minds in history. I'll warn you, some of this may be somewhat controversial.

How to Wake Up with More Energy (On Less Sleep)

Through experimenting with various sleep durations of his own—as well as learning those of many other Miracle Morning practitioners who have tested this theory—Hal found that how our sleep affects our biology is largely influenced by our personal *belief* about how much sleep we need. In other words, how we feel when we wake up in the morning—and this is a very important distinction—is not solely based on how many hours of sleep we got but rather significantly impacted by how we told ourselves we were going to feel when we woke up.

For example, if you *believe* that you need eight hours of sleep to feel rested, but you're getting into bed at midnight and have to wake up at 6:00 a.m., you're likely to tell yourself, "Geez, I'm only going to get six hours of sleep tonight, but I need eight. I'm going to feel exhausted in the morning." Then, what happens as soon as your alarm clock goes off and you open your eyes and realize it's time to wake up? What's your first thought? It's the same thought you had before bed! "Geez, I only got six hours of sleep. I feel exhausted." It's a self-fulfilling, self-sabotaging prophecy. If you tell yourself you're going to feel tired in the morning, then you are going to feel tired. If you believe that you need eight hours to feel rested, then you're not going to feel rested on anything less. But what if you changed your beliefs?

The mind-body connection is a powerful thing, and I believe we must take responsibility for every aspect of our lives, including the power to wake up every day feeling energized, regardless of how many hours of sleep we get.

So, how many hours of sleep do you *really* need? You tell me. If you struggle with falling or staying asleep, and it is a concern for you, I highly recommend getting a copy of Shawn Stevenson's book, *Sleep Smarter: 21 Essential Strategies to Sleep Your Way to a Better Body, Better*

Health, and Bigger Success. It's one of the best, most well-researched books that I've seen on the topic of sleep.

3. Rest to Recharge

The conscious counterpart to sleep is *rest.* While some people use the terms interchangeably, they're quite different. You might get eight hours of sleep, but if you spend all of your waking hours on the go, then you won't have any time to think or recharge your physical, mental, and emotional batteries. When you work all day, run from activity to activity after hours, and then finish with a quick dinner and a late bedtime, you don't allow for a period of rest.

Likewise, spending weekends taking the kids to soccer, volleyball, or basketball, then heading out to see a football game, going to church, singing in the choir, attending several birthday parties, etc., can do more harm than good. While each of these activities is great individually, maintaining a fully-packed schedule doesn't allow for time to recharge.

We live in a culture that perpetuates the belief that when our days are busy and exciting, we are more valuable, more important, or more alive. In truth, we are all of those things when we can be at peace within our own skin. Despite our best intentions to live balanced lives, the modern world demands that we are almost always connected and productive, and these demands can drain us emotionally, spiritually, and physically.

What if, instead of being constantly on the go, you valued intentional quiet time, sacred space, and periods of purposeful silence? How might that improve your life, your physical and emotional well-being, and your ability to achieve entrepreneurial success?

It may seem counterintuitive to take time out when your to-do list is a mile long, but the fact is that more rest is a prerequisite to productive work.

Research proves that rest melts your stress away. Practices like yoga and meditation also lower heart rates, blood pressure, and oxygen consumption, along with alleviating hypertension, arthritis, insomnia, depression, infertility, cancer, and anxiety. The spiritual benefits of resting are profound. Slowing down and getting quiet means you can tap into your inner wisdom, knowledge, and voice. Rest and its close sibling, relaxation, allow us to reconnect with the world around us, inviting ease and a sense of contentment into our lives.

And yes, in case you're wondering, you'll be more productive, nicer to your friends and family members (not to mention your colleagues, employees, and clients), and in general much happier as well. When we rest, it's like letting the earth lie fallow rather than constantly planting and harvesting. Our personal batteries need to be recharged. The best way is to recharge them is to truly and simply rest.

Easy Ways to Rest

Most of us confuse rest with recreation. To rest, we do things like hike, garden, work out, or even party. Any of these activities can only be termed restful because they are breaks from work; but truthfully, they are not, and cannot, be defined as rest.

Rest has been defined as a kind of waking sleep, experienced while you are alert and aware. Rest is the essential bridge to sleep, and we achieve rest and sleep the same way: by making space for them and allowing them to happen. Every living organism needs rest, including you. When we don't take the time to rest, eventually its absence takes a toll on the body. Below are a few easy ways to start getting the rest your body needs.

- If you are now investing five or ten minutes each morning, during your S.A.V.E.R.S., to meditate or sit in silence, that is a great start.

- You can reserve Sundays or, if Sunday is a busy workday for you, choose another day of the week for rest. You can spend time alone, reading or watching a movie, or do something low-key with family, like cooking a meal together, playing games with your kids, and enjoying each other's company.

- When you're driving, drive in silence: turn off the radio and stow your phone.

- Go for a walk without your earbuds in. Even a walk in nature without intention or goals, such as burning calories, can work.

- Turn off the television. Designate a half hour, an hour, or even half a day for silence. Try taking a few conscious breaths, during which you focus on your inhale and exhale or the space between breaths.

- Mindfully drink a cup of tea, read something inspirational, write in your journal, take a hot bath, or get a massage.

- Attend a retreat. It could be with your team, a group of friends, your church, any community with which you are involved, family, your spouse, or on your own in nature.

Even taking a nap is a powerful way to rest and recharge. If I'm feeling drained during the day for some reason and still have long hours ahead, I won't hesitate to hit the reset button with a twenty- or thirty-minute power nap. Napping also can lead to better sleep patterns.

It's helpful to set a specific time for rest. Put boundaries around it so you can claim that time.

The Rest Habit

As an entrepreneur, you're in the trenches by default. You'll need to schedule your time for rest and self-care in the same way you schedule the other appointments in your life. The energy you get back will reward you many times over.

Rest certainly isn't something we were taught in school, and it may not come naturally at first. After all, you're a driven, hard-charging entrepreneur. So, you may find that you consciously need to make it a priority. Learning different mindfulness techniques and bringing them into your everyday life is an effective way to deeply rest your body, mind, and spirit. Practices such as mid-day meditation, yoga, and purposeful silence are powerful ways to go within and achieve restful states of being, particularly when you commit to practicing them regularly.

The more you integrate periods of rest and silence into your daily life, the bigger the payoff will be. During more tranquil periods, perhaps you won't need to rest as much, but periods of intensity (such as meeting a huge quota or a big deadline) may require more rest and silence than usual.

Combining exercise, healthy food choices, consistent sleep, and rest will give you a quantum leap in the right direction for you and your business. Keep in mind that when you try to adopt these three practices—to eat, sleep, and rest more effectively—you may at first find them to be uncomfortable. Your mind and body may encounter some emotional resistance. Resist the urge to run from discomfort by committing to a healthier life.

Putting Energy Engineering into Action

Step One: Commit to eating and drinking for energy by prioritizing the consequences of the foods you eat above the taste. After your initial glass of water in the morning, ingest some form of healthy fat to fuel your brain. Try incorporating one new healthy meal, made up of *living* foods, into your diet each day. Instead of snacking on potato chips, try kale chips or fresh organic fruit. And remember to keep a full bottle of water with you all the time to stay hydrated.

Step Two: Sleep and wake to win by committing to a consistent daily bedtime *and* wake-up time. Based on what time you wake up to do your Miracle Morning, determine what time you'll go to bed to ensure that you will get enough rest. Maintain a specific bedtime for a few weeks to get your body acclimated. If you need a little nudge to get to bed on time, remember to set a recurring bedtime alarm that prompts you to start winding down one hour before it's lights out. After a couple of weeks, feel free to play with the number of hours you leave for sleeping to optimize your energy levels.

Step Three: Incorporate time into your daily calendar to rest and recharge, whether that includes meditating, taking a nap, going for a walk, or doing anything that gives you joy and rejuvenation. Remember, Hal takes a two-hour lunch break every day, which gives him time to either play basketball or wakeboard—two activities that he loves to do and that thoroughly reenergize him. Which activities can you plan into your day that will reenergize you? In addition to your Miracle Morning routine, schedule regular daily periods to rest and recharge.

Now that you have a plan for your body let's direct our attention to your focus.

෴

Morning Millionaires

TIM FERRISS, the bestselling author of *The 4-Hour Workweek,* starts his day by making his bed, then meditating for ten to twenty minutes. He follows that with a brief period of light exercise, then journals for five to ten minutes.

12

Not-So-Obvious Millionaire Principle #3:

UNWAVERING FOCUS

The successful warrior is the average man, with laser-like focus.
BRUCE LEE, world-renowned martial artist and actor

W e've all met that person. You know—*that* person. The one who runs marathons, coaches Little League, volunteers at her son's school lunch program, and maybe writes a novel on the side. And on top of all that? She's an incredible entrepreneur, getting tons of press, winning awards, and knocking it out of the park when it comes to growing her business, year after year. I bet you know someone like that—someone who seems unbelievably, inexplicably *productive.*

Or maybe you know *this* person: the entrepreneur who runs a million-dollar-plus business but never seems to be working in it. He's always playing golf or out on the lake, even in the middle of the workweek. Every time you see him, he's talking either about the vacation he just got back from or the one he's getting ready to leave for. He's fit, always happy, and makes every person he encounters feel like a million bucks.

You might know both those people, but what you might not know is how they do it. Maybe you always thought she was lucky. Or gifted. Or perhaps you thought he was connected. Or had the right personality. Or was born with superpowers.

While those things can help when it comes to achieving millionaire status, I know from experience that the real superpower behind every unbelievably productive person is their *unwavering focus*. Unwavering focus is the ability to maintain clarity about your highest priorities and to take all the energy you've learned to generate for yourself, channel it into what matters most, and keep it there, regardless of what is going on around you or how you feel. This ability is key to becoming an exceptional performer.

Focus is another form of leveraging your time—just like prioritizing, as we discussed in "Lesson 4: Becoming Super." When you harness the power of focus, you don't become superhuman, but you can achieve seemingly superhuman results. And the reasons for this are surprisingly straightforward.

- **Unwavering focus makes you more effective.** Being effective doesn't mean doing the most things or doing things the fastest. It means doing the *right* things. It means you engage in the activities that create forward momentum toward your life's goals.

- **Unwavering focus makes you more efficient.** Being efficient means doing things with the fewest resources, such as time, energy, or money. Every time your mind wanders away from your goals, you waste those things—particularly time. In pursuit of our goals, time is always in demand, so every moment that your focus wavers is another moment lost.

- **Unwavering focus makes you productive**. Understand that, just because you're *busy* does not mean you are productive. In fact, those who are struggling financially are frequently the busiest. Too often we confuse being busy—engaged in activities that don't produce results, like checking emails or cleaning your car or reorganizing your to-do list for the twelfth time this month—with being productive. When you have a clear vision, identify your highest priorities, and consistently execute your most leveraged activities, you'll go from being busy to being productive. By taking the steps that we're about to cover, you'll learn how to develop the habit of unwavering focus and join the ranks of the most productive people in the world.

If you combine those benefits, you will achieve *a lot* more. Perhaps the greatest value of focus, however, is that rather than scattering your energy across multiple areas of your life and getting mediocre results across the board, you will release untapped potential *and* improve your life.

Now let's turn your Miracle Morning to the task. Here are four steps you need to follow up your Miracle Morning with sustained focus.

1. Find Your Best Environment(s) for Unwavering Focus

Let's start here: *you need an environment that supports your commitment to unwavering focus.* It might be your spare bedroom, or it could be your backyard. No matter how modest, though, you need a place where you go to focus.

Part of the reason for this is simple logistics. If your materials are scattered from the trunk of your car to the kitchen counter, you can't be effective. A bigger reason, however, is that **having a place where you focus triggers the habit of focusing.** Sit at the same desk to do great work at the same time every day, and soon enough you'll find yourself slipping into the zone just by sitting down in that chair.

If you travel a lot, then your car, your suitcase, your hotel rooms, and possibly random coffee shops are part of your focus space too. Build habits for how you pack and work on the road, and you can trigger great focus the same way you do at the office. When you are prepared and always have exactly what you need with you, you can work anywhere.

2. Clear the Unfocused Clutter

Clutter is a focus killer, and tackling it is our next stop on the journey. There is a reason that Marie Kondo's book, *The Life-Changing Magic of Tidying Up*, is one of the best-selling non-fiction books of the last decade; decluttering both your physical and mental space will inspire a calm, motivated mindset.

There are two kinds of clutter: mental and physical, and we all have them both. We carry around scattered thoughts in our minds, like these: *My sister's birthday is coming up. I should get her a gift and card. I had a great time at dinner the other night. I need to send the host a thank-you note. I must answer the email from my new client before I leave the office today.*

Then there are the physical items we accumulate: stacks of paper, old magazines, sticky notes, clothes we never wear, the pile of junk in the garage. The trinkets, knick-knacks, and tokens that accumulate as we go through life.

Clutter of either type creates the equivalent of heavy fog; to become focused, you need to be able to *see*. To clear your vision, you'll want to get those items out of your head and collected so you can relieve the mental stress of trying to remember them. And then, you'll want to get those physical items out of your way.

Here's a simple process to help you clear the fog and create the clarity you need to focus.

- **Create a master to-do list.** You probably have lots of things you haven't written down yet—start with those. Add the contents of all those sticky notes that clutter your desk, computer screen, planner, countertops, and refrigerator (are there other places?). Put those notes and action items on your master list in one central location, whether that's a physical journal or a list on your phone so that you can clear your mental storage. Feeling better? Keep going; we're just getting started.

- **Purge your workspace.** Schedule a half (or full) day to go through every stack of paper, file folder stuffed with documents, and tray full of unopened mail—you get the gist. Throw out or shred what you don't need. Scan or file the ones that matter. Note in your journal any items that need your attention and cannot be delegated, then pick a time in your schedule to complete them.

- **Declutter your life.** Wherever possible, clean up and clear out every drawer, closet, cabinet, or other space that doesn't give you a sense of calm and peace when you see it. This includes your car interior and trunk. This might take a few hours or a few days. Schedule a short time each day until everything is complete. Saying, "I just need a weekend to declutter," is a sure way to never start. Pick a single drawer and start there. You'll be surprised at how the little bursts of work accumulate. Try S.J. Scott and Barrie Davenport's book, *10-Minute Declutter: The Stress-Free Habit for Simplifying Your Home*, for suggestions.

Getting physically and mentally organized will allow you to focus at a level you would never believe possible. It leaves your energy with nowhere to go except toward what *matters*.

3: Protect Yourself from Interruptions

In addition to running my core businesses, I'm writing this book, and am also married with kids. As you can imagine, my time is critically important to me, just as I'm sure yours is to you.

To avoid distraction and ensure that my attention is focused on the task at hand, my phone is almost always set on Do Not Disturb mode. This blocks all incoming calls, texts, or notifications like email and social media. This is a simple thing that dramatically increases my daily productivity and ability to remain focused on the task at hand. I recommend returning phone calls and emails at pre-designated times, according to your schedule, not everybody else's.

You can apply the same philosophy and strategies to any notifications, alerts, and/or social media updates, as well as your availability for colleagues, employees, and even clients. Do Not

Disturb isn't just a setting on your phone. Let your team know when you're available and when they need to leave you undisturbed.

4. Build a Foundation for Unwavering Focus

Once you identify your focus place and begin the process of decluttering your life, you should experience a remarkable increase in focus from clearing the fog in your mind.

Now, it's time to take things to the next level. I use three questions to improve my focus.

- What's working that I should *keep doing* (or do more of)?
- What do I need to *start doing* to accelerate results?
- What do I need to *stop doing* immediately that's holding me back from going to the next level?

If you can answer those three questions and act on the answers, you'll discover a whole new level of productivity you probably didn't think was possible. Let's look at each question in detail.

What Do You Need to *Keep Doing* (or Do More of)?

Let's face it, not all tactics and strategies are created equal. Some work better than others. Some work for a while and then become less effective. Some even make things worse.

Right now, you're probably doing a lot of the right activities, and you'll be nodding right along as you read the coming sections. If you already know the things you're doing that are working, jot those down. Perhaps you're already using the Do Not Disturb function, or you're already well into a fitness challenge and feeling stronger each day, for example. Put that on the "what's working" list.

Make sure you're choosing things that contribute to increasing your success as a whole. Make sure that the activities you're doing are directly related to becoming more successful. Consider the 80/20 rule (originally the Pareto principle), which shows that roughly 80 percent of our results come from 20 percent of our efforts. Which 20 percent of your activities impact 80 percent of your results? It's easy to keep the things that you *like* doing, but this is reality—you need to make sure that the activities you're doing are directly related to the business at hand, as well as putting money in your bank account.

At the end of this chapter, you'll have an opportunity to capture in your journal the activities that are working. (Among them, I hope, will be that you've started doing the Life S.A.V.E.R.S.) Everything that's on that list is a *keep doing* until it's replaced by something even more effective.

For each of the "keep doing" activities on your list, make sure you're completely honest with yourself about *what you need to be doing more of* (in other words, what you're currently not doing enough of). If it's something you think you should be doing but it's not moving you forward toward your important goals, it doesn't belong on your list. Perfection is not one of the goals here. Overworking yourself is ultimately unproductive and takes your focus off the important things.

Keep doing what's working and, depending on how much more you want to achieve, do *more* of what's working.

What Do You Need to *Start* Doing?

Once you've captured what's working and determined what you need to do more of, it's time to decide what else you can do to accelerate your success.

I have a few top-shelf suggestions to prime the pump and get you started.

- Review your goals and plans for creating wealth as discussed in "Lesson 3: Your Flight Plan."

- Understand your financial position on a daily and weekly basis—both your personal finances and any business activity.

- Exercise regularly.

- Eat foods that energize you and help you maintain good health.

- Build good habits around sleep and rest, as per the energy engineering chapter.

- Consider what activities you *aren't* doing that would directly impact your income or business profit.

- Plan your first, or next, hire. This could be a personal assistant, a virtual assistant, or an intern. Realize that hiring someone to free up your time is an *investment*, not an expense.

- Create your *foundational schedule*—that recurring, ideal weekly schedule with a time-blocked calendar, as discussed in "Not-So-Obvious Millionaire Principle #1: Self-Leadership."

I caution you not to become overwhelmed here. Keep in mind that Rome wasn't built in a day. You don't need to identify fifty-eight action items and implement them by tomorrow. The great thing about having a daily scribing practice as part of your Miracle Morning means you can capture everything you wish to do. Then, one or two at a time, add them to your success toolbox until they become habits. Incremental improvements have a magical way of accumulating.

What Do You Need to *Stop* Doing?

By now, you've most likely added a few items to start doing. If you're wondering where the time is going to come from, this might be your favorite step of all. It's time to let go of the things you've been doing that don't serve you to make room for the ones that do.

I'm sure you complete a number of daily activities you will be relieved to stop doing, thankful to delegate to someone else, or grateful to release altogether.

Why not stop:

- Eating unhealthy, energy-draining foods that suck the life and motivation out of you?

- Doing unnecessary household chores?

- Replying to texts and emails instantly?

- Answering the phone? (Let it go to voicemail and reply when the timing works best for you.)
- Reading and posting on social media sites?
- Watching hours of television a day?
- Beating yourself up or worrying about what you can't change?
- Doing repetitive tasks such as paying the bills, buying groceries several times a week, or even cleaning your house?

Or, if you want to improve your focus dramatically in one simple step, try this easy fix: *stop responding to electronic buzzes like a trained seal.* Do you really need to be alerted every time you receive texts, emails, and social media notifications? I didn't think so. Go into the settings of your phone, tablet, and computer and turn all your notifications OFF.

Technology exists for your benefit, and you can take control of it this very minute. How often you check your phone messages, texts, and email can and should be decided by *you*. Let's face it, most of us do not have jobs that will result in a life-or-death situation if we do not respond immediately to a call, text, or email. We don't need to be accessible 24/7/365 except to our significant others and our children. In fact, most smartphones now come with the option to silence all calls *except* for individuals that you pre-determine, such as your family members. An effective alternative is to schedule times during the day to check on what's happening, what needs your immediate attention, and what items can be added to your schedule or master to-do list and what can be deleted, ignored, or forgotten.

Final Thoughts on Unwavering Focus

Focus is like a muscle that you build over time, and it's a muscle that is directly relevant to building wealth. Every millionaire I know has developed the ability to focus, and the ones who struggle with attention have all not only practiced techniques to improve but have hired people to help them stay on track and undistracted when they need it most.

Like with any muscle, you need to show up and do the work to make your ability to focus grow. Cut yourself some slack if you falter and keep pushing forward. It will get easier. It might take you time to learn to focus, but every day that you try, you'll continue to get better at it. Ultimately, this is about *becoming* someone who focuses, which starts with seeing yourself as such. I recommend that you add a few lines to your affirmations about your commitment to unwavering focus and what you will do each day to develop it.

Most people would be shocked to discover just how little time they spend on important, relevant activities each day. Today, or in the next twenty-four hours, schedule sixty minutes to focus on the *single most important task you have*, and you'll be amazed not only by your productivity but also by how empowering it feels.

By now, you've added some pretty incredible action items and focus areas to your success arsenal. After you complete the steps below, head into the next section, where we will sharpen your wealth-creation skills and combine them with the Life S.A.V.E.R.S. in ways you might not have heard about or thought of before! Remember the steps we discussed in this chapter on the importance of unwavering focus and the ways to increase it in your life.

Putting Unwavering Focus into Action

Step One: Choose or create your ideal environment to support unwavering focus. If your focus is optimum when you're working in a public place, such as a coffee shop, schedule focused time-blocks at Starbucks. If you work from home, make sure you've implemented step two, below.

Step Two: Clear your physical and mental clutter. Start by scheduling a half day to clean up your workspace. Then, clear your mind with a brain dump. Unload all those little to-do lists floating around in your head. Create a master to-do list, either on your computer, on your phone, or in your journal.

Step Three: Protect yourself from interruptions, both from yourself—by turning off notifications—and from others, by putting your phone into Do Not Disturb mode and letting your circle of influence know to leave you alone during your focused time-blocks.

Step Four: Start building your unwavering focus lists. Pull out your journal, or open a note on your phone or computer, and create the following three lists:

- **What I need to keep doing (or do more of).**
- **What I need to start doing.**
- **What I need to stop doing.**

Begin jotting down everything that comes to mind. Review your lists and determine which activities can be automated, outsourced, or delegated. How much time do you spend on your top business-growth and income-producing activities? Repeat these questions until you are clear on what *your* process is and start time-blocking your days so that you're spending close to 80 percent of your time on tasks that produce results. Delegate the rest.

You've now got a great handle on how to incorporate the Life S.A.V.E.R.S. into your work and personal life in a way that will touch every part of your world. Millionaire or not, you'll begin to thrive by setting aside time each morning to put these not-so-obvious principles to work.

Now it's time to look in detail at the essential attributes of millionaires and how mornings can help you bring them into your life.

ᘓ

Morning Millionaires

AUBREY MARCUS, CEO of Onnit begins the first 20 minutes of each day with water, light, and movement.

As described in his bestselling book, *Own the Day, Own Your Life*, he starts the day with his Morning Mineral Cocktail to hydrate and replenish minerals lost during sleep, which consists of 12 ounces of filtered water, 3 grams of sea salt, and ¼ lemon, squeezed.

Next, he exposes himself to blue-light in order to set his circadian rhythms, either directly from the sun or from a blue-light device, such as Valkee's Human Charger.

Finally, he moves his body through exercise, for as little as one minute, to wake up the internal systems that will enable him to perform at his best and own the day.

THE 30-DAY MIRACLE MORNING CHALLENGE

THE THREE PHASE STRATEGY TO IMPEMENT ANY HABIT IN ONE MONTH

"Life's too short" *is repeated often enough to be a cliché, but this time it's true. You don't have enough time to be both unhappy and mediocre. It's not just pointless; it's painful.*

-SETH GODIN, *New York Times* bestselling author

L et's play devil's advocate for a moment. Can *The Miracle Morning* transform any area of your life or business in just thirty days? Can anything make that significant of an impact that quickly?

To begin, consider that it has already done that for thousands of others. If it works for them, it can and will work for you.

Incorporating or changing any habit does require an acclimation period, so don't expect this to be effortless from day one. However, if you commit to yourself to stick with it, beginning each day with a Miracle Morning and the S.A.V.E.R.S. will quickly become the foundational habit that makes all other changes possible. Remember: win the morning, and you set yourself up to win the day.

The seemingly unbearable first few days of habit change are only temporary. While there's a lot of debate about how long it takes to implement a new habit, the hundreds of thousands of people who have learned how to conquer the snooze button, and now wake up every day for their Miracle Morning, can testify to the following three-phase strategy.

From Unbearable to Unstoppable:

The Three-Phase Strategy to Implement Any Habit in Thirty Days

The following approach is arguably the simplest and most effective strategy to implement and sustain a new habit in just thirty days. It will give you both the mindset and the roadmap to build your new routine.

Phase One: Unbearable (Days One to Ten)

Any new activity requires greater conscious effort in the beginning and getting up early is no different. In Phase One, you're fighting existing morning habits that have been entrenched in who you are for years, and that's going to take some willpower on your part.

In this phase, it's mind over matter—and if you don't mind, it will definitely matter! The habit of hitting the snooze button and missing out on every morning is the same habit that holds you back from becoming the superstar you have always known you can be. So, dig in and hold strong.

While you battle existing patterns and limiting beliefs in this phase, you'll also find out what you're made of and what you're capable of. You need to keep pushing, stay committed to your vision, and hang in there. Trust me, and thousands of other newly-minted morning people, when we say *you can do this.*

I know from experience that it can be daunting on day five to realize you still have twenty-five days to go before your transformation is complete and you've become a bona fide morning person. But keep in mind that on day five, you're more than halfway through the first phase. You're well on your way. Remember: your initial feelings are not going to last forever. You owe it to yourself to persevere; in no time at all, you'll be getting the exact results you want as you become the person you've always wanted to be!

Phase Two: Uncomfortable (Days Eleven to Twenty)

Welcome to Phase Two, where your body and mind begin to acclimate to waking up earlier. You'll notice that getting up starts to get a tiny bit easier, but it's not yet a habit—it's not quite who you are, and it likely won't feel natural yet.

The biggest temptation at this point is to reward yourself by taking a break, especially on the weekends. However, taking Saturday and Sunday off to sleep in will only make it more difficult for you when Monday comes—particularly when you're just starting out.

A question posted quite often in The Miracle Morning Community is, "How many days a week do you get up early for your Miracle Morning?" The most common answer from people is consistently along the lines of: *I started by taking the weekend off. But when I would wake up late on the first Saturday and Sunday mornings, I felt like I had wasted what would have been a productive Miracle Morning. So, now I do it seven days a week.*

Ultimately, there's no pressure here. Do what's right for you and focus on *progress* over perfection.

The best part of Phase Two is that Phase One is over. You've made it through the hardest period, so keep going. Why on earth would you want to go through that first phase again by taking one or two days off? Trust me; you wouldn't. So, don't. Hang tough, stay committed.

Phase Three: Unstoppable (Days Twenty-One to Thirty)

By now, early rising is now not only a habit, but it has become part of who you are, part of your identity. Your body and mind will have become accustomed to your new way of being. These next ten days are important for cementing the habit in yourself and your life.

As you engage in the Miracle Morning practice, you'll also gain a perspective on these three distinct phases of habit change. That means you can now identify and adopt any habit that serves you—including the habits of the morning millionaires that we have included in this book.

Now that you've learned the simplest and most effective strategy for successfully implementing and sustaining any new habit in thirty days, you know the mindset and approach that you need to complete The 30-Day Miracle Morning Challenge. All that's required is for you to commit to starting and following through.

Consider the Rewards

When you commit to The 30-Day Miracle Morning Challenge, you'll build a foundation for success in every area of your life, for the rest of your life. By waking up each morning and practicing the Miracle Morning, you begin each day with extraordinary levels of discipline (the crucial ability to get yourself to follow through with your commitments), clarity (the power you'll generate from focusing on what's most important), and personal development (perhaps the single most significant determining factor in your success). In the next thirty days, that foundation will help you become the person you need to be to create the extraordinary levels of personal, professional, and financial success you desire.

You'll also be transforming the Miracle Morning from a concept that you may be excited (and possibly a little nervous) to "try" into a lifelong habit that will continue to develop you into the person you need to be to create the life you've always wanted. You'll begin to fulfill your potential and see results in your life far beyond what you've ever experienced before.

In addition to developing successful habits, you'll also be cultivating the mindset you need to improve your life—both internally and externally. By practicing the Life S.A.V.E.R.S. each day, you'll be experiencing the physical, intellectual, emotional, and spiritual benefits of Silence, Affirmations, Visualization, Exercise, Reading, and Scribing. You'll immediately feel less stressed and more centered, focused, happy and excited about your life. You'll be generating more energy, clarity, and motivation to move toward your highest goals and dreams (especially those you've been putting off far too long).

Remember, your life will improve after—but only after—you develop yourself into the person you need to be in order to improve it. That's exactly what these next thirty days of your life can be—a new beginning, and a new you.

You Can Do This!

If you're feeling nervous, hesitant, or concerned about whether or not you can follow through with this for thirty days, relax—it's completely normal to feel that way. This is especially true if waking up in the morning is something you've found challenging in the past. In fact, it's not only normal to be a bit hesitant or nervous, but it's a very good sign! It's an indicator that you're ready to commit; otherwise, you wouldn't be nervous.

Here's how to get started.

Step 1: Get The Miracle Morning 30-Day Life Transformation Challenge Fast Start Kit

Visit www.TMMBook.com to download your free Miracle Morning 30-Day Life Transformation Challenge Fast Start Kit—complete with the exercises, affirmations, daily checklists, tracking sheets, and everything else you need to make starting and completing The Miracle Morning 30-Day Life Transformation Challenge as easy as possible. Please take a minute to do this now.

Step 2: Plan Your First Miracle Morning for Tomorrow

If you haven't already begun, commit to (and schedule) your first Miracle Morning as soon as possible—ideally tomorrow. Yes, actually write it into your schedule and decide where it will take place. Remember, it's recommended that you leave your bedroom as soon as you wake up and remove yourself from the temptations of your bed altogether. My Miracle Morning takes place every day on my living room couch while everyone else in my house is still sound asleep. I've heard from people who do their Miracle Morning sitting outside in nature, such as on their porch or deck, or at a nearby park. Do yours where you feel most comfortable, but also where you won't be interrupted.

Step 3: Read Page One of the Fast Start Kit and Do the Exercises

Read the introduction in your Miracle Morning 30-Day Life Transformation Challenge Fast Start Kit, then please follow the instructions and complete the exercises. Like anything in life that's worthwhile, successfully completing The Miracle Morning 30-Day Life Transformation Challenge requires a little preparation. It's important that you do the initial exercises in your Fast Start Kit (which shouldn't take you more than an hour). Keep in mind that your Miracle Morning will always start with the preparation you do the day or night before to ready yourself mentally, emotionally, and logistically for your Miracle Morning. This preparation includes following the steps in The Five-Step Snooze-Proof Wake-Up Strategy in Chapter 2.

Step 3.1: Get an Accountability Partner

The overwhelming evidence for the correlation between success and accountability is undeniable. While most people resist being held accountable, it is hugely beneficial to have someone who will hold us to higher standards than we'll hold ourselves to. All of us can benefit from the support of an accountability partner. It's highly recommended—but not required—that you reach out to someone in your circle of influence (family, friend, colleague, significant other, etc.) and invite them to join you in The Miracle Morning 30-Day Life Transformation Challenge.

Not only does having someone to hold us accountable increase the odds that we will follow through, joining forces with someone else is more fun! Consider that when you're excited about something and committed to doing it on your own, there is a certain level of power in that excitement and in your individual commitment. However, when you have someone else in your life—a friend, family member, or co-worker—who is as excited about and committed to it as you are, it's much more powerful.

Call, text, or email one or more people today, and invite them to join you for The Miracle Morning 30-Day Life Transformation Challenge. The quickest way to get them up to speed is to send them the link to www.MiracleMorning.com so they can get free and immediate access to The Miracle Morning Fast Start Kit, including:

- The FREE Miracle Morning video training
- The FREE Miracle Morning audio training
- Two FREE chapters of *The Miracle Morning* book

It will cost them nothing, and you'll be teaming up with someone who is also committed to taking their life to the next level; the two of you can offer support, encouragement, and accountability to each other.

IMPORTANT: Don't wait until you have an accountability partner on board to do your first Miracle Morning and start The 30-Day Life Transformation Challenge. Whether or not you've found someone to embark on the journey with you, I still recommend scheduling and doing your first Miracle Morning tomorrow—no matter what. Don't wait. You'll be even more capable of inspiring someone else to do the Miracle Morning with you if you've already experienced a few days of it. Get started. Then, as soon as you can, invite a friend, family member, or co-worker to visit www.MiracleMorning.com to get their free Miracle Morning Fast Start Kit.

In less than an hour, they'll not only be fully capable of being your Miracle Morning accountability partner but probably a little inspired to improve their own lives.

Are You Ready to Take Your Life to the Next Level?

What is the next level in your personal or professional life? Which areas need to be transformed in order for you to reach that level?

Give yourself the gift of investing just thirty days to make significant improvements in your life, one day at a time. No matter what your past has been, you can change your future by changing the present.

CONCLUSION
THE TRADE

*Every success story is a tale of
constant adaption, revision, and change.*

-RICHARD BRANSON,
billionaire founder of The Virgin Group

There are a lot of things I didn't start out as. Here's a short list:

- Wealthy
- Goal-seeking
- Proactive
- Organized
- Productive
- An early riser

There's much more I could add to that list, but the point is this: as a young man, I was far from ideally positioned to become a millionaire. When I look back at my younger self, it's with a strange mix of humor and shock. Sometimes I find it hard to believe, when I look at my life now, that I'm the same person.

There's no way, for example, that my younger self would have woken up this morning before his alarm went off—never mind before the sun! There's also no way that a youthful version of me would have sat down immediately after waking and gone through the S.A.V.E.R.S.

It also seems, at first glance, like there's no way that same young man would become very wealthy.

But I did. I became wealthy as surely as I did the S.A.V.E.R.S. this morning.

Reality Check

For those who are wondering: I don't masterfully execute a perfect Miracle Morning routine 365 days a year. I'm not a morning ninja or a super-guru. I'm just a guy with a deep interest in trying to improve myself.

I probably nail my "ideal" routine about 100 days of the year. The rest of the days, I hit some variation of it—an abbreviated Miracle Morning of sorts. Occasionally, stuff happens, and I don't have anything even *close* to a Miracle Morning. On those days, it feels like some sort of miracle when I finally crawl into bed at night.

On those days, however, I'm also reminded of a truth that's easy to forget: *days are fragile things.*

If I lose control of the morning, I'll often lose control of the day. Things snowball. My mood and energy shift. I never quite catch up and never quite feel that sense of calm that I get when I start the day on my terms, in a space of peace and control.

I don't like that feeling of losing a day. After all, how many do I have? I don't know, but I do know that we all get fewer than we wish for.

And so, on a day when things seem to fall apart, I close my eyes and tell myself, *tomorrow morning will be different.*

And you know what? It usually is. That reminder—that a day, a morning, a *life*, is a fragile thing—is enough to get me right back to my Miracle Morning where I'm at my best.

The point is this: *you don't have to be perfect.* In fact, you probably shouldn't even try. What you *should* do is try to get better. To continually improve both the quality *and* the quantities of your Miracle Mornings. Just a little each day.

Just like compound interest, it adds up to big things in the end.

Your Journey to Wealth

If the bottom line isn't already clear, here it is again: you don't become a millionaire *just* by waking up early. Plenty of hardworking people wake up early their whole lives and never even manage to own their own home. Waking up early doesn't guarantee wealth any more than opening a bank account does.

Yet, the Miracle Morning works. The S.A.V.E.R.S. work. The strategies in this book for building a mindset for wealth *work*. It all works.

Here's why.

Becoming wealthy is a journey. That may sound cliché, but it's true. Very few people become wealthy overnight, and those who do often suffer greatly. Most sustainable, enjoyable wealth comes from a journey—a process over time.

There are some obvious signposts on that journey—things like starting a business, or buying a rental property, or learning to manage and leverage your money. But those signposts are just the outward signs of something deeper. They're the visible indicators of *personal growth.*

Look all you want, but I don't believe it's possible to find a self-made millionaire who hasn't developed themselves. They've all been on the same journey you're embarking on: the journey of self-improvement and learning. When I look back at my younger self, I realize, of course, that I am the same person. I've just gotten *better.*

When I think over the years since I began my journey to wealth, I realize that I've made a trade. I've exchanged the old me—the one who slept in and procrastinated—for a new me. The same me, inside, but I've traded up to a newer model. The *me* of years ago just had much to learn. Thanks to the power of mornings, I was able to do that learning. I was able to give up who I was for who I could become.

And that, in a nutshell, is why the Miracle Morning works: because it gives you both the time *and* the process for *creating a better you*. It allows you to trade who you are right *now* for who you can *become*.

Mornings are the ultimate equalizer. We all have different strengths. We all have different talents, backgrounds, advantages, and disadvantages. But what we all share is that we each get one morning a day. As long as you live, without fail, you get one morning a day.

Those mornings can help you create the life of your dreams, or you can dream your life away. The choice is up to you.

Fortunately, tomorrow morning isn't far off. What choice will you make?

To your happiness, health, and wealth.

—David Osborn

A SPECIAL INVITATION FROM HAL

Readers and practitioners of *The Miracle Morning* have co-created an extraordinary community consisting of over 150,000 like-minded individuals from around the world who wake up each day *with purpose* and dedicate time to fulfilling the unlimited potential that is within all of us, while helping others to do the same.

As author of *The Miracle Morning*, I felt that I had a responsibility to create an online community where readers could come together to connect, get encouragement, share best practices, support one another, discuss the book, post videos, find an accountability partner, and even swap smoothie recipes and exercise routines.

However, I honestly had no idea that The Miracle Morning Community would become one of the most positive, engaged, and supportive online communities in the world, but it has. I'm constantly astounded by the caliber and the character of our members, which presently includes people from over seventy countries and is growing daily.

Just go to **www.MyTMMCommunity.com** and request to join The Miracle Morning Community on Facebook. You'll immediately be able to connect with 150,000+ people who are already practicing TMM. While you'll find many who are just beginning their Miracle Morning journey, you'll find even more who have been at it for years and will happily share advice, support, and guidance to accelerate your success.

I moderate the Community and check in regularly, so I look forward to seeing you there! If you'd like to connect with me personally on social media, just follow **@HalElrod** on Twitter and **Facebook.com/YoPalHal** on Facebook. Let's connect soon

BONUS CHAPTER
THE MIRACLE EQUATION
BY HAL ELROD

There are only two ways to live your life.
One is as though nothing is a miracle.
The other is as though everything is a miracle.

-ATTRIBUTED TO ALBERT EINSTEIN

You understand now that you can wake up early, maintain extraordinary levels of energy, direct your focus, and master the millionaire lessons from David Osborn. If you also apply what follows to every aspect of your life, you're going to go much further: you're going to make your life truly exceptional.

There is one more helpful tool for you to add to your tool-box and help you make this leap, and it's called The Miracle Equation.

The Miracle Equation is the underlying strategy that I used to realize my full potential as a salesperson, as well as a friend, spouse, and parent. And it has to do with how you handle your goals. One of my mentors, Dan Casetta, taught me: "The purpose of a goal isn't to hit the goal. The real purpose is to develop yourself into the type of person who can achieve your goals, regardless of whether you hit that particular one or not. It is who you become by giving it everything you have until the last moment—regardless of your results—that matters most."

When you decide to stick with a seemingly unachievable goal, despite the fact that the possibility of failure is high, you will become especially focused, faithful, and intentional. When your objective is ambitious, it will require you to find out what you are made of!

Two Decisions

As with any great challenge, you need to make decisions related to achieving the goal. You can set a deadline and then create your agenda by asking yourself, "If I were to achieve my goal on the deadline, what decisions would I have to make and commit to in advance?"

And you'll find that whatever the goal, the two decisions that would make the biggest impact are always the same. They form the basis for The Miracle Equation.

The First Decision: Unwavering Faith

There was a time in my life when I was trying to achieve an impossible sales goal. Though this example comes from my business experience, I'll show you how it applies to any context. It was a stressful time, and I was already facing fear and self-doubt, but my thought process about the goal forced me to an important realization. *To achieve the seemingly impossible, I would have to maintain unwavering faith every day, regardless of my results.*

I knew that there would be moments when I would doubt myself and times when I would be so far off track that the goal would no longer seem achievable. And it would be those moments when I would have to override self-doubt with unshakeable faith.

To keep that level of faith in those challenging moments, I repeated what I call my Miracle Mantra:

I will _____ (reach my goal), no matter what. There is no other option.

Understand that maintaining unwavering faith isn't normal. It's not what most people do. When it doesn't look like the desired result is likely, average performers give up the faith that it's possible. When the game is on the line, a team is down on the scorecards, and there are only seconds left, it is the top performers—the Michael Jordans of the world—who, without hesitation, tell their team, "Give me the ball."

The rest of the team breathes a sigh of relief because they're freed from their fear of missing the game-winning shot, while Michael Jordan is backed by a decision made at some point in his life that he would maintain unwavering faith, despite the fact that he might miss. (And although Michael Jordan missed twenty-six game-winning shots in his career, his faith that he would make every single one never wavered.)

That's the first decision that very successful people make, and it's yours for the making, too.

When you're working toward a goal, and you're not on track, what is the first thing that goes out the window? The faith that the outcome you want is possible. Your self-talk turns negative: *I'm not on track. It doesn't look like I'm going to reach my goal.* And with each passing moment, your faith decreases.

You don't have to settle for that. You have the ability and the choice to maintain that same unwavering faith, no matter what, regardless of the results. This is key in building wealth because results are often out of your direct control. You may doubt yourself or have a bad day at work or in business. In the darkest moments, you may wonder if everything will turn out okay. But you must find—over and over again—your faith that all things are possible and hold it throughout your journey, whether it is a thirty-day sales goal or a thirty-year business career.

It's very important that you see your role in building wealth as directly related to other high-achieving professions because the parallels are unmistakable. If you don't take time to see the parallels here, you may find that you focus on the failures of your path instead of the successes.

Elite athletes maintain unwavering faith that they can make every shot they take. That faith—and the faith you need to develop—isn't based on probability. It comes from a whole different place. Most salespeople operate based on what is known as the law of averages. But what we're talking about here is the law of miracles. When you miss shot after shot, you need to tell yourself what a world-class athlete tells him/herself: *I will make the next shot, no matter what. There is no other option.*

And if you miss that one, your faith doesn't waver. You repeat the Miracle Mantra to yourself:

I will _____ [insert your goal], no matter what. There is no other option.

Then, you uphold your integrity and do what it is that you say you are going to do.

An elite athlete may be having the worst game ever, where it seems like in the first three-quarters of the game, they can't make a shot to save their life. Yet in the fourth quarter, right when the team needs them, they start making those shots. They always want the ball; they always have belief and faith in themselves. In the fourth quarter, they score three times as many shots as they scored in the first three-quarters of the game.

Why? They have conditioned themselves to have unwavering faith in their talents, skills, and abilities, regardless of what it says on the scoreboard or their stats sheet.

They also combine their unwavering faith with part two of The Miracle Equation: extraordinary effort.

The Second Decision: Extraordinary Effort

When you allow your faith to go out the window, effort almost always follows right behind it. After all, you tell yourself, what's the point in even trying to achieve your goal if it's not possible? Suddenly, you find yourself wondering how you're ever going to get out of debt or break even in your business, let alone reach the big goal you've been working toward.

I've been there many times, feeling deflated, thinking, *What's the point of even trying?* And you might think: *There's no way I can make it. My finances are headed in the wrong direction.*

That's where extraordinary effort comes into play. You need to stay focused on your original goal and to connect to the vision you had for it, that big why in your heart and mind when you set the goal in the first place.

You need to reverse engineer the goal. Ask yourself: *If I'm at the end of this month and this goal were to have happened, what would I have done? What would I have needed to do?*

Whatever the answer, you will need to stay consistent and persevere, regardless of your results. You have to believe you can still ring the bell of success at the end. You have to maintain unwavering faith and extraordinary effort until the buzzer sounds. That's the only way that you create an opportunity for the miracle to happen.

If you do what the average person does—what our built-in human nature tells us to do—you'll be just that: average. Don't choose to be that average person! Remember: your thoughts and actions create your results and are therefore a self-fulfilling prophecy. So, manage them wisely.

Allow me to introduce you to your edge—the strategy that will practically ensure every one of your goals is realized.

The Miracle Equation

Unwavering Faith + Extraordinary Effort = Miracles

It's easier than you think. The secret to maintaining unwavering faith is to recognize that it's a mindset and a strategy—it's not concrete. In fact, it's elusive. No salesperson makes every sale. You can never sink every shot. You can never win every battle in business or work—or at home, for that matter. So, you have to program yourself to have the unwavering faith to drive you to keep putting forth the extraordinary effort regardless of the results.

Remember, the key to putting this equation into practice, to maintaining unwavering faith in the midst of self-doubt, is the Miracle Mantra:

I will _____, no matter what. There is no other option.

Once you set a goal, put that goal into the Miracle Morning format. Yes, you're going to say your affirmations every morning (and maybe every evening, too). But all day, every day, you're going to repeat your Miracle Mantra to yourself. As you're driving the kids to school or taking the train to the office, while you're on the treadmill, in the shower, in line at the grocery store—in other words: everywhere you go.

Your Miracle Mantra will fortify your faith and be the self-talk you need to make just one more attempt, try after try.

Bonus Lesson

Remember what I learned from my mentor Dan Casetta on the purpose of goals? You have to become the type of person who can achieve the goal. You won't always reach the goal, but you can become someone who maintains unwavering faith and puts forth an extraordinary effort, regardless of your results. That's how you become the type of person you need to become to achieve extraordinary goals consistently. What a great lesson for your children!

And while reaching the goal almost doesn't matter (almost!), more often than not, you will reach your goal. Do the elite athletes win every time? No. But they win most of the time. And you'll win most of the time, too.

You can wake up earlier; do the Life S.A.V.E.R.S. with passion and excitement; get organized, focused, and intentional; and master every financial challenge like a champ. And yet, if you don't combine unwavering faith with extraordinary effort, you won't reach the levels of success you seek.

The Miracle Equation gives you access to forces outside of anyone's understanding, using an energy that I might call God, the Universe, the Law of Attraction, or even good luck. I don't know how it works; I just know that it works.

You've read this far—you clearly want success more than almost anything. Commit to following through with every aspect of your millionaire journey, including The Miracle Equation. You deserve it, and I want you to have it!

Putting It into Action

1. Write out The Miracle Equation and put it where you will see it every day: Unwavering Faith + Extraordinary Effort = Miracles (UF + EE = M∞)

2. Decide your number one goal for your wealth journey this year. What goal, if you were to accomplish it, would bring you closest to your ideal life?

3. Write your Miracle Mantra: I will _____ (insert your goals and daily actions here), no matter what. There is no other option.

It is more about who you become in the process. You'll expand your self-confidence and, regardless of your results, the very next time you attempt to reach a goal, and every time after that, you'll be the type of person who gives it all they've got.

Closing Remarks

Congratulations! You have done what only a small percentage of people do: read an entire book. If you've come this far, that tells me something about you: you have a thirst for more. You want to become more, do more, contribute more, and earn more.

You have the unprecedented opportunity to infuse the Life S.A.V.E.R.S. into your daily life and business, upgrade your daily routine, and ultimately upgrade your life to a first-class experience beyond your wildest dreams. Before you know it, you will be reaping the astronomical benefits of the habits that top achievers use daily.

Five years from now, your family life, business, relationships, and income will be a direct result of one thing: who you've become. It's up to you to wake up each day and dedicate time to becoming the best version of yourself. Seize this moment in time, define a vision for your future, and use what you've learned in this book to turn your vision into your reality.

Imagine a time just a few years from now when you come across the journal you started after completing this book. In it, you find the goals you wrote down for yourself—dreams you didn't dare speak out loud at the time. And as you look around, you realize your dreams now represent the life you are living.

Right now, you stand at the foot of a mountain you can effortlessly climb. All you need to do is continue waking up each day for your Miracle Morning and use the Life S.A.V.E.R.S. day after day, month after month, year after year, as you continue to take yourself, your family, and your success to levels beyond what you've ever experienced before.

Combine your Miracle Morning with a commitment to master the lessons of the wealthy and use The Miracle Equation to create results that most people only dream of.

This book was written as an expression of what we know will work for you, to take every area of your life to the next level, faster than you may currently believe possible. Miraculous performers weren't born that way—they have dedicated their lives to developing themselves and their skills to achieve everything they've ever wanted.

You can become one of them, I promise.

Taking Action: The 30-Day Miracle Morning Challenge

Now it is time to join the tens of thousands of people who have transformed their lives with the Miracle Morning. Join the community online at TMMBook.com and download the toolkit to get started today

ENDNOTES

Morning Millionaire Routines

Richard Branson

https://virgin.com/richard-branson/why-i-wake-up-early

Arianna Huffington

https://mymorningroutine.com/arianna-huffington/

Howard Schultz

https://bloomberg.com/news/articles/2012-04-12/how-to-make-coffee-at-home-howard-schultz

Steve Jobs

http://independent.co.uk/news/business/news/from-steve-jobs-obama-jeff-bezos-mark-zuckerberg-how-8-of-the-world-s-most-successful-people-start-a6686466.html

Daymond John

https://medium.com/personal-growth/how-to-plan-your-ideal-year-2d12ff073467

Oprah Winfrey

https://inc.com/bryan-adams/6-celebrity-morning-rituals-to-help-you-kick-ass.html

Barbara Corcoran

https://www.huffingtonpost.com/entry/10-morning-routines-of-wildly-successful-entrepreneurs_us_58a0c97fe4b080bf74f03dd8

Jack Dorsey

https://www.inc.com/dave-schools/exactly-how-much-sleep-mark-zuckerberg-jack-dorsey-and-other-successful-business.html

Ryan Holiday

https://ryanholiday.net/my-morning-routine/

Tim Ferriss

https://inc.com/bryan-adams/6-celebrity-morning-rituals-to-help-you-kick-ass.html

Aubrey Marcus

Book, *Own the Day, Own Your Life* (Harper Wave - April 17, 2018)

ABOUT THE AUTHORS

HAL ELROD is on a mission to *Elevate the Consciousness of Humanity, One Morning at a Time.* As one of the highest rated keynote speakers in the America, creator of one of the fastest growing and most engaged online communities in existence and author of one of the highest rated books in the world, *The Miracle Morning*—which has been translated into 27 languages, has over 2,000 five-star Amazon reviews and is practiced daily by over 500,000 people in 70+ countries—he is doing exactly that.

The seed for Hal's life's work was planted at age twenty when Hal was found dead at the scene of a horrific car accident. Hit head-on by a drunk driver at seventy miles per hour, he broke eleven bones, died for six minutes, and suffered permanent brain damage. After six days in a coma, he woke to face his unimaginable reality—which included being told by doctors that he would never walk again.

Defying the logic of doctors and proving that all of us can overcome even seemingly insurmountable adversity to achieve anything we set our minds to, Hal went on to not only walk but to run a 52-mile ultramarathon and become a hall of fame business achiever—all before the age of 30.

Then, in November of 2016, Hal nearly died again. With his kidneys, lungs, and heart of the verge of failing, he was diagnosed with a very rare, very aggressive form of leukemia and given a 30% chance of living. After enduring the most difficult year of his life, Hal is now cancer-free and furthering his mission as the Executive Producer of *The Miracle Morning* movie, a documentary about morning rituals.

Most importantly, Hal is beyond grateful to be sharing his life with the woman of his dreams, Ursula Elrod, and their two children in Austin, Texas.

For more information on Hal's keynote speaking, live events, books, the movie and more, visit www.HalElrod.com.

DAVID OSBORN is the principal owner of the sixth largest real estate company in the U.S., with over 4,500 agents responsible for more than 34,000 transaction sides and an excess of $10 billion in sales in 2017. In addition to being a primary investor or operator of more than thirty-five profitable real estate-related businesses and the Co-Founder & Chairman of Magnify Capital, he currently does or has done, business in more than forty U.S. states and Canada. He's also the *New York Times* bestselling author of *Wealth Can't Wait*.

Firmly rooted in the principle of knowledge sharing and giving back, David is a founder and operating partner of GoBundance, an accountability-based group of hard-charging, generous entrepreneurs living exceptional lives. Further, David sits on the boards of the One Life Fully Lived nonprofit and Habitat for Humanity Austin and is a member of TIGER 21. He contributes to various causes—from fighting cancer to building clean-water wells through charity: water to helping lift women and children out of poverty in Ethiopia through A Glimmer of Hope to making sure little humans get more than a little care at Dell Children's Hospital.

David is the proud father of two beloved daughters and one amazing son and is married to the wonderful and talented Traci Osborn. For more information on David's books, Keynote Speaking and more please visit www.DavidOsborn.com.

HONORÉE CORDER is the author of dozens of books, including *You Must Write a Book, The Prosperous Writers* book series, *Like a Boss* book series, *Vision to Reality, Business Dating, The Successful Single Mom* book series, *If Divorce is a Game, These are the Rules,* and *The Divorced Phoenix.* She is also Hal Elrod's business partner in *The Miracle Morning* book series. Honorée coaches business professionals, writers, and aspiring non-fiction authors who want to publish their books to bestseller status, create a platform, and develop multiple streams of income. She also does all sorts of other magical things, and her badassery is legendary. You can find out more at HonoreeCorder.com.

THE MIRACLE MORNING SERIES

The Journal

for Salespeople

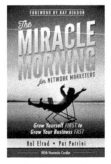

for Real Estate
Agents

for Network
Marketers

for Writers

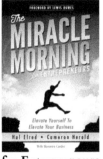

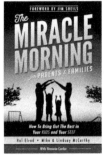

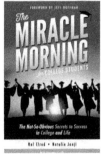

for Entrepreneurs

for Parents &
Families

for College
Students

COMPANION GUIDES & WORKBOOKS

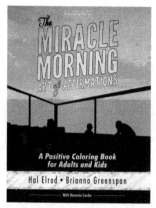

Art of Affirmations

for Network Marketers
90-Day Action Plan

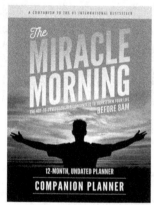

Companion Planner

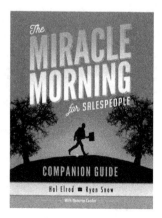

for Salespeople
Companion Guide

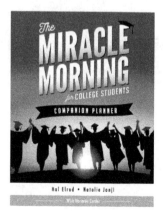

for College Students
Companion Planner

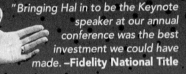

CPSIA information can be obtained
at www.ICGtesting.com
Printed in the USA
LVHW02s1740220818
587769LV00013B/659/P